STRENGTH UNDER CONTROL

**Bert Ghezzi and Peter Williamson
General Editors**

Strength Under Control

Meekness and Zeal in the Christian Life

John Keating

SERVANT BOOKS
Ann Arbor, Michigan

Published by Servant Books
        P.O. Box 8617
        Ann Arbor, Michigan 48107

Cover photo by H. Armstrong Roberts
Book design by John B. Leidy

Scripture quotations are taken from the *Revised Standard Version*, copyright 1946, 1953, © 1971, 1973 by the Division of Christian Education of the National Council of Churches of Christ in the U.S.A.; the *New International Version*, copyright © 1978 by New York Bible Society, all rights reserved; *The New American Bible*, copyright © 1970 by the Confraternity of Christian Doctrine, Washington, D.C., all rights reserved; *The New Oxford Annotated Bible*, copyright © 1962 and © 1965 by Oxford University Press, Inc.

Printed in the United States of America.

ISBN 0-89283-104-9

Contents

Living as a Christian

In human terms, it is not easy to decide to follow Jesus Christ and to live our lives as Christians. Jesus requires that we surrender our selves to him, relinquish our aspirations for our lives, and submit our will to God. Men and women have never been able to do this easily; if we could, we wouldn't need a savior.

Once we accept the invitation and decide to follow Jesus, a new set of obstacles and problems assert themselves. We find that we are often ignorant about what God wants of us as his sons and daughters. For example, what does it mean practically to obey the first commandment — to love God with our whole mind, heart, and strength? How can we know God's will? How do we love people we don't like? How does being a Christian affect what we do with our time and money? What does it mean "to turn the other cheek?" In these areas — and many others — it is not easy to understand exactly what God wants.

Even when we do know what God wants, it can be quite difficult to apply his teaching to our daily lives. Questions abound. How do we find time to pray regularly? How do we repair a relationship with someone we have wronged or who has wronged us?

How do we handle unruly emotional reactions? These are examples of perplexing questions about the application of Christian teaching to our daily lives.

Furthermore, we soon discover that Christians have enemies — the devil outside and the flesh within. Satan tempts us to sin; our inner urges welcome the temptation, and we find our will to resist steadily eroding.

Finally, we must overcome the world. We are trying to live in an environment that is hostile toward what Christians believe and how they live and friendly toward those who believe and do the opposite. The world in which we live works on our Christian resolve in many subtle ways. How much easier it is to think and act like those around us! How do we persevere?

There is a two-fold answer to these questions: To live successfully as Christians, we need both grace and wisdom. Both are freely available from the Lord to those who seek him.

As Christians we live by grace. The very life of God works in us as we try to understand God's teaching, apply it to our lives, and overcome the forces that would turn us aside from our chosen path. We always need grace, and grace is always there. The Lord is with us always, and the supply of his grace is inexhaustible.

Yet grace works with wisdom. Christians must *learn* a great deal about how to live according to God's will. We must study God's word in scripture, listen to Christian teaching, and reflect on our own experience and the experience of others. Many Christians today lack this kind of wisdom. This is the need which the *Living as a Christian* series is designed to meet.

The book you are reading is part of a series of books intended to help Christians apply the teaching of scripture to their lives. The authors of *Living as a Christian* books are pastoral leaders who have given this teaching in programs of Christian formation in various Christian communities. The teaching has stood the test of time. It has already helped many people grow as faithful servants of the Lord. We decided it was time to make this teaching available in book form.

All the *Living as a Christian* books seek to meet the following criteria:

- **Biblical.** The teaching is rooted in scripture. The authors and editors maintain that scripture is the word of God, and that it ought to determine what Christians believe and how they live.

- **Practical.** The purpose of the series is to offer down-to-earth advice about living as a Christian.

- **Relevant.** The teaching is aimed at the needs we encounter in our daily lives — at home, in school, on the job, in our day-to-day relationships.

- **Brief and Readable.** We have designed the series for busy people from a wide variety of backgrounds. Each of the authors presents profound Christian truths as simply and clearly as possible, and illustrates those truths by examples drawn from personal experience.

- **Integrated.** The books in the series comprise a unified curriculum on Christian living. They do not present differing views, but rather they take a consistent approach.

The format of the series makes it suitable for both individual and group use. The books in *Living as a Christian* can be used in such group settings as Sunday school classes, adult education programs, prayer groups, classes for teen-agers, women's groups, and as a supplement to Bible study.

The *Living as a Christian* series is divided into several sets of books, each devoted to a different aspect of Christian living. These sets include books on Christian maturity, emotions in the Christian life, the fruit of the Holy Spirit, Christian personal relationships, Christian service, and very likely, on other topics as well.

This book, *Strength Under Control*, is part of a set that deals with Christian character. One of the goals of our Christian life is to become more like Jesus. We all know words, such as loving, meek, and joyful, that describe the qualities of Jesus. But we need help, not only in determining what these marks of character are but also in knowing how to grow in them. *Strength Under Control* and other books in this set define the elements of Christian character and teach Christians how to be transformed in the Lord's image and likeness.

The editors dedicate the *Living as a Christian* series

to Christian men and women everywhere who have counted the cost and decided to follow Jesus Christ as his disciples.

Bert Ghezzi and Peter Williamson
General Editors

ONE

A Case for Christian Character

I have a friend who has immigrated to the United States from Europe. He has become an American citizen and has learned to speak English and to conduct himself in American society. He has even mastered a fair amount of American slang. Yet, my friend still seems pretty un-American. He has a strong foreign accent. He dresses a little differently. His sense of humor is somewhat different, and he is puzzled at times by American jokes. Although he is an American citizen, my friend still reflects a different national character.

In some ways, we Christians can be like my friend. Through baptism and faith in Christ, we have become citizens of a new nation—God's nation. We have learned certain essentials that allow us to live successfully among this new people: things like sound doctrine and good morals. Yet at the same time, many traits of our previous national character—that of fallen, unredeemed humanity—continue to cling to us. They are not so major as to invalidate our citizenship, but they make us seem like foreigners who have only recently immi-

grated. In America, having a foreign national character is certainly not a moral problem—in fact, it
need not be a problem at all. In the kingdom of
God, however, a foreign character is a very real
problem, for the character of the nation is God's
own character as he has revealed it in Jesus Christ,
and he wants all of his people to bear it proudly.

We Christians tend to neglect the importance
that God places on our characters. Living the
Christian life is a far more glorious call than we
often imagine. For God's intention is to restore us
fully to his image and likeness, to make us "chips
off the old block." And this has implications. It
means that we must be concerned with more than
believing the right things and obeying certain commands. We must also *be the right thing*—from the
inside out. As a result, although we all have quite
different personalities, certain qualities of character should typify all Christians. *holiness*

Taking on God's Character

Though it often goes unnoticed, the New Testament lays out some specific instructions about
Christian character. It frequently recommends a
number of qualities to which we should aspire.
Among them are such godly virtues as love, joy,
peace, patience, kindness, generosity, reliability,
meekness, self-control, compassion, zeal, forbearance, and perseverance.

It is not at all easy to grow into God's character
and to become increasingly like Jesus Christ—
acting and responding as he would. But that is the

goal that lies before us if we will pursue it. The temptation is always to resist, to stop short of all that God intends to do in us. His process of reforming us is often uncomfortable and at times quite painful. It's easy for us to settle for less. Our justification might go something like this: "Well, there are some pretty sizable discrepancies between Jesus' character and mine, but my faults and character defects aren't *that* major, and besides, nobody's perfect. Sure, I can get pretty grouchy and irritable at times, and that streak of selfishness and lack of generosity doesn't show any signs of going away. And I've got to learn to control my tongue better, because it gets me into trouble at times. But, that's the way I am, and I've learned to accept myself and be content."

But should we be so easily contented? More of our faults and defects can change than we might imagine, if we will cooperate with God's grace at work in us. He has a great and splendid plan for us and is not likely to settle for less, provided that we don't. The holiness of our characters is a high priority for him. If we will allow it, he will never cease working to bring us to perfection. C. S. Lewis has aptly described God's work of building our characters this way:

Imagine yourself as a living house. God comes in to rebuild that house. At first, perhaps, you can understand what He is doing. He is getting the drains right and stopping the leaks in the roof and so on: you knew that those jobs needed doing and so you are not surprised. But presently He starts knocking the house about in a way that hurts abominably and does not seem to make sense. What on earth is He up to? The explanation is that He is building quite a different house from the one you thought of—throwing out a new wing here, putting on an extra floor there, running up towers, making courtyards. You thought you were going to be made into a decent little cottage: but He is building a palace. He intends to come and live in it Himself.

Growing fully into the character of God, into his image and likeness, is a lifelong project. In fact, it will never be completed on this side of the grave. But God's upward call will lead us daily into a richer and better life, into becoming more like his Son Jesus, true children of our Father in heaven.

Meekness and Zeal

My earlier list of New Testament character traits is by no means exhaustive. But I will not be so ambitious as to attempt to cover even that selected list in one short book. My aim is more modest and specific: to look at two traits—meekness and zeal—which are regularly underrated and misunderstood today, yet which are of prime importance to a Christian in our own day and age.

Why are meekness and zeal so important for us? One could cite a number of reasons. The first is quite simple. God clearly ascribes great value to them. They are qualities of God himself, and scripture indicates that they are essential equipment for a Christian who wants to be like his Lord, responding to the people and circumstances of daily life as Jesus would. This fact alone is reason enough to make meekness and zeal virtues worth striving for.

There are other reasons as well. A second is that these two qualities bear directly on a very prominent concern of people in our society—the question of personal style. Many people today are very self-conscious about their "style"—that is, the deliberately chosen image they would like to project, which entails a particular manner of relating to others. "I like your style" is an exalted compliment these days. Among the styles most in vogue at present are the "cool," "laid-back," indifferent, and inexpressive style, especially admired among young people, and the hard, confronting, aggressive style popularized by such movements as student activism, black power, women's liberation, and gay liberation in the sixties and seventies. These reigning styles can look appealing to Christians, who at times embrace them wholeheartedly, without noticing how seriously these styles diverge from the model of behavior set by Jesus and taught by the New Testament. Christian qualities like meekness and zeal have a great deal to say about our "personal style," if we will listen.

Third, far more than mere personal style is at stake in taking on such Christian traits as meekness and zeal. Their development in us will markedly affect the way we live. Our daily behavior and our relationships with others will be powerfully influenced as these qualities take hold in our characters. A brief look at some scenes from daily life might highlight their impact.

Jim and Sarah Marshall are up late on a Friday evening preparing for their vacation. Residents of Pittsburgh, they plan to pack up the car and their three young children early the next morning and head down to Virginia to visit Jim's parents. But they are not of one mind about the trip. Jim wants to drive all the way through. Sarah wants to stop overnight at a motel. "Jim, you know what happens on these long rides. The kids get restless and cranky, then you get angry, and then we're all miserable. Besides, I really dislike long drives."

Unfortunately for Sarah, her husband loves long drives. And he doesn't want to spend any more vacation time than necessary just getting there and back. "You know where we're at with the budget this month, honey. We really shouldn't spend money on a motel if we can avoid it." Both Jim and Sarah have good reasons for their positions. Both also hold some strong opinions and clear personal preferences. An argument ensues.

This kind of scene is common in the life of a family. There are, of course, two reasonable sides to the issue. The manner in which Jim and Sarah go about resolving such daily disputes will say a great deal about the success of their marriage, the strength and peace of their family life, and their enjoyment of the vacation. Here the virtue of meekness on Jim's and on Sarah's part would be of enormous value.

Steve Shorter is a freshman at State University. He is a dedicated Christian, but he finds that his beliefs are often not respected. In the classroom and in his dormitory, God, his Son Jesus, and the Christian faith are frequently subject to ridicule. His philosophy professor takes an entire class period to speak against the existence of God, scolding and challenging those students who believe in God. Several men in his dorm hold a mock funeral for a dead mouse, aping a Christian preacher, and belittling the Bible and the Christian hope in the resurrection.

What do we do when the truths of our faith come under fire? Do we respond differently than when we ourselves are the objects of attack? Once again, a key to sorting out such issues and making a strong Christian response lies in our understanding the role of zeal and meekness.

Elaine Caruso is an executive secretary in a large Dallas firm. She has been on the job for a few years, and she is an excellent secretary: efficient, hard-working, and well-organized. However, she is not particularly well-paid. It's about time, she decides, to ask for that long-overdue raise. Her boss, however, is a skinflint. He is also an avid believer in the most recent intimidation techniques, and he immediately suspects her intentions when she asks if she can speak to him this morning. He takes the initiative as she enters his office by criticizing her appearance and her recent work. Then glancing deliberately at his watch, he growls, "Now, I'm in a hurry. What the devil do you want?"

If we are good Christians like Elaine, how should we deal with confrontation, conflict, and injustice in resolving issues like these—issues that face us daily, and to which we should aim to respond as Christ himself would? In all of these cases, it is not merely a matter of responding according to our personality or our emotional state, or of acting in the manner most calculated to get us what we want. Rather at issue is our living as God's true sons and daughters, who respond to people and events according to our nature.

To Be a Servant

All along, I have spoken of meekness and zeal in tandem, as though they were related. One might very reasonably ask: What has humble, lowly meekness to do with bold, aggressive zeal? How can you speak of them together, except as polar opposites that must somehow both fit into a Christian's life? In this book I hope to show that, as paradoxical as it might at first appear, meekness and zeal are quite intimately related. They are like two sides of the same coin.

And what sort of unusual coin is that? It is one of the most priceless treasures in the storehouse of Christian virtue, a quality central to the character and identity of Jesus: the quality of Christian servanthood. This rare and precious quality is so foundational to meekness and zeal, and so essential if we are to become like the Lord, that we must begin by taking a careful look at Jesus' words on servanthood. From there, we can proceed to more specific and pointed questions. What is true Christian meekness? And what is Christian zeal? How were these qualities manifested in Christ's life, and what are they to look like in ours? And how does this Christian ideal of meek and zealous servant-hood stack up against the prevailing ideals and personal styles of the secular world in which we live?

The answers to these questions can be life-changing. My own life has been profoundly affected as I have discovered the true meaning of Christian meekness and zeal, and of the New Testament's instruction on Christian character in general. The call to imitate Christ, to live as sons and daughters of God, is truly a high one—the highest call in life. Those who accept its full challenge will not be disappointed, in this life or the next.

TWO

Who Is the Greatest?

As C. S. Lewis noted earlier, building Christian character bears some similarities to building a house. A crucial principle of building is to begin with a solid foundation. The rooms on the first floor can only be properly constructed if they rest securely on the house's well-laid foundation. Similarly, the qualities of meekness and zeal must be firmly established on the broader base of Christian servanthood—a fundamental Christian quality of which they are important facets—if they are to develop and come to full maturity in us. Our growth in meekness and zeal must begin with hearing and embracing Jesus' call to Christian servanthood. In this chapter, we will look at Jesus' challenging teachings on being a servant. Then, in chapters three and four, we will examine how Christian servanthood finds expression in meekness and zeal.

Jesus said that whoever humbled himself like a child would be called great in the kingdom of heaven. Let us look at the context in which he made this statement.

The appointed time was drawing near. Aware of the events to come, Jesus had been earnestly instructing his disciples in the secrets of the kingdom of God. Soon he would be leaving Galilee for the last time, heading for Jerusalem and the trials awaiting him there. His disciples were huddled together, vigorously discussing a matter of vital concern to them all. Unable to resolve the issue among themselves, they brought it to Jesus.

At that time the disciples came to Jesus, saying, "Who is the greatest in the kingdom of heaven?" And calling to him a child, he put him in the midst of them, and said, "Truly, I say to you, unless you turn and become like children, you will never enter the kingdom of heaven. Whoever humbles himself like this child, he is the greatest in the kingdom of heaven" (Mt 18:1-4).

At first glance, it might appear from the disciples' question that they were eagerly turning their minds to lofty and distant thoughts of the future life, contemplating the heavenly existence of the age to come. Not so. Their question was very practical. It had immediate bearing on all their lives. To understand why this is so, we must take a closer look at the meaning of their question.

An Earthly Kingdom

First of all, their question concerned the "kingdom of heaven." Most of us reading these lines would tend to think immediately of that place outside of space and time where God dwells in all his splendor and glory, seated upon his royal throne, surrounded by all his heavenly host. To the disciples in the Gospel of Matthew, who were asking this question, however, this phrase meant something quite different. It referred to that same reality which in the gospels of Mark and Luke is called "the kingdom of God." Understanding what that phrase ("the kingdom of heaven"/"the kingdom of God") meant to the Jewish people of Jesus' day will make clear the real question that lay behind the disciples' query.

For the meaning of that phrase stirred the Jews greatly. It meant glory for the nation of Israel. It meant freedom from their hated oppressors. It meant the total and ultimate triumph of God over his enemies. For all these things the people of Israel fervently longed, and they firmly believed that the day was coming when all would come to pass.

Much of their hope was based upon their faith in the fulfillment of the prophecy of Isaiah:

> It shall come to pass in the latter days
> that the mountain of the house of the Lord
> shall be established as the highest of the
>   mountains,
> and shall be raised above the hills;
> and all the nations shall flow to it,
> and many peoples shall come, and say:
> "Come, let us go up to the mountain of the
>   Lord,
> to the house of the God of Jacob;
> that he may teach us his ways

and that we may walk in his paths."
For out of Zion shall go forth the law,
and the word of the Lord from Jerusalem.
He shall judge between the nations,
and shall decide for many peoples;
and they shall beat their swords into
    plowshares,
and their spears into pruning hooks;
nation shall not lift up sword against nation,
neither shall they learn war any more.

O house of Jacob,
come, let us walk
in the light of the Lord (Is 2:2-5).

Israel had always understood this prophecy, and
others like it, to be foretelling the glorious kingdom of God on earth. It would be established "in
the latter days," inaugurating the everlasting reign
of God over his people and over all the nations of
the earth. God would rule the world, through his
anointed king (Messiah) from the holy city of Jerusalem. Every chain of oppression would be
smashed, and there would never again be war on
the face of the earth. Israel would then be in its
glory, and all the peoples of the earth would come
to it, to pay homage to the Lord and to learn his
ways and his law.

Israel's eager expectation and longing for the
fulfillment of this prophecy had been greatly intensified in the recent years before Jesus' appearance.
In 63 B.C. the great Roman general Pompey had
annexed the land of Israel for the Empire, a great

blow to national pride, but more importantly, a serious threat to religious freedom. For a while, the Jews were permitted their own rulers, but in 6 A.D. Archelaus, the son of Herod the Great, was deposed from the rule in Jerusalem, and the first Roman procurator was sent in his place. The people of Israel were outraged that they were forced to submit to direct government by pagans, who neither understood nor believed their faith. They chafed bitterly under the often cruel regime of the procurators, and their anger fanned the flames of desire and expectation to fever pitch. Surely, many said, the coming of the Messiah, the destruction of the hated Romans, and the establishment of God's kingdom were close at hand.

The Preaching of John and Jesus

The stage was now set for the appearance of John the Baptist, and then Jesus, proclaiming in power for all of Israel to hear, "Repent, for the kingdom of heaven is at hand!" (Mt 3:2; 4:17). Their message was certainly one of "good news," for it struck the most resonant chord in the hearts of the people. Great furor was generated by their preaching, and many fervently hoped, first of John and then of Jesus, that the Messiah had finally come and would soon begin the work of inaugurating his kingdom.

These ideas were very much alive in the minds of the Twelve, who had begun as followers of John (Jn 1:35-42; Acts 1:21-22), and had turned to follow Jesus, whom they believed to be the Messiah. Now

they had been with him for three years. They had
heard his public and private teaching. They had
seen incredible works of power performed at his
hands. There could no longer be any doubt. Here,
indeed, as Peter had only recently proclaimed, was
"the Christ [Messiah], the Son of the living God"
(Mt 16:16).

And now Jesus was telling them that the time
was at hand. They were going up to Jerusalem.
True, he was saying some disturbing and utterly
incomprehensible things about suffering and dy-
ing, but these had not really registered with the
disciples. All they knew was that Jesus would soon
declare his kingdom and establish his royal throne
in Jerusalem. And there with him would be his
twelve closest disciples, at his side as his most
trusted and powerful ministers.

All this was very thrilling, but one unresolved
issue ate away at their excitement and disturbed
their brotherly harmony. Which of them was to be
the top man in Jesus' kingdom? Who among them
would enjoy the highest privilege of sitting beside
Jesus, wielding the greatest power and authority
in the realm? It was much on their minds, a source
of tension and rivalry among them. They decided
to take it up with the Lord himself.

Becoming Like Children

Jesus listens to their question with patience. He
knows that they have not yet understood much of
what he has taught them, and probably will not
until he has died and risen. Now he takes the

opportunity to teach them how different his kingdom is from the one they have in mind. He shows them what true greatness consists of in the eyes of God. His answer takes them completely by surprise. "Unless you turn and become like children, you will never enter the kingdom of heaven. Whoever humbles himself like this child, he is the greatest in the kingdom of heaven" (Mt 18:3-4).

What an amazing statement! What could Jesus mean by requiring his disciples to "become like children?"

Many people today suggest that Jesus is speaking of the qualities of young children, recommending them to us for our instruction and imitation. Jesus is telling us, they say, to be like children in their innocence, charm, simplicity, trustfulness, spontaneity, and creativity. According to this interpretation, these are the qualities that God most values and looks for in his children, qualities which open the way for one's entrance into the kingdom of heaven.

Is this really what Jesus means to say? I think not, for several reasons. First of all, this meaning of the response would not really answer the disciples' question. Once we have understood the actual point of their question and what "greatness" signifies to them, it becomes obvious that this interpretation of Jesus' answer doesn't even address their concern. They are asking about position and power, while Jesus extolls childlike creativity, spontaneity, and charm.

Second, it is hard to imagine that Jesus, the bold and powerful proclaimer of the gospel of the kingdom, is here carefully instructing his disciples that childlike simplicity and innocence are the core of his gospel, the very heart of the Christian life, without which one "will never enter the kingdom of heaven." These qualities may have real value, but it is highly doubtful that they are central virtues to which all Christians should aspire.

3)   What is more, the picture of children defined by this constellation of virtues suffers from a serious, even fatal flaw: it is false. It is idealized, sentimentalized, and one-sided. The full panorama of childlike character—the bad as well as the good—is sadly lacking in this romantic portrait. It is certainly true that children can be innocent, creative, imaginative, spontaneous, joyful, and fun-loving. It is just as true, however, that they can be selfish, irresponsible, greedy, deceitful, jealous, and cruel. Like the adults they will eventually become, children are beset with all the human frailty and sin that results from the Fall. The little girl of nursery-rhyme fame (the one with the little curl in the middle of her forehead) is a fair representation of the average child: "When she was good, she was very, very good, but when she was bad, she was horrid."

I have firsthand experience to back up my statements, having been a child myself once. By and large I was a "good kid," raised in a fine Christian home, and taught right from wrong at an early age. From that same early age, though, I was fully capable of cruelty and treachery in my dealings with my younger brothers and sisters, often taking full advantage of my age, size, and experience.

The same was true of my friends. Like typical kids, we were quick to gang up on an outcast, quick to ridicule and mock. One such example has been firmly fixed in my mind. I was in the second grade. A few years ahead of me, in the fifth grade, was a boy with one of the worse cases of acne I've ever seen. The boys in the school dubbed him "Pizza Face," and taunted him mercilessly about it. One day on the playground, I and my second-grade cohorts began to tease him. After suffering taunts for a while, he lashed out in his frustration and rage and grabbed the first little kid he could get his hands on: me. I thought for sure I was done for, and braced myself for the thrashing that I deserved. I didn't get it, though. For some reason, he just gripped me hard and slammed his hand over my mouth to shut me up. My friends and I should have learned something that day. But all we really learned was to stay outside of arm's reach when mocking someone bigger and stronger than we.

Now, I was not an exceptionally bad child. In fact, I might even have been considered an exceptionally good one at times. But along with a measure of goodness I had the capacity to be pretty bad. And so it is with most children. It is hard to imagine that Jesus would have displayed such poor judgment about human nature as to miss this fact. It would make more sense to conclude that he was not speaking of character when he recommended the imitation of children to his disciples.

There is a further reason why this modern, sentimental interpretation of Jesus' words seems unlikely. The romantic, idealized view of children is a relatively recent development, a few hundred years old at most. To speak of children in these terms in first-century Palestine would have completely mystified Jesus, his disciples, and any bystanders who would have chanced to hear. Their own understanding of children, one which makes perfect sense of the words of Jesus, ran along a completely different line from the modern, romantic portrait. It had to do, not with children's character or behavior, but with their *position*.

Children in Israel

What was the position of children in first-century Palestine? The answer to this question will shed great light on the perplexing words of Jesus. A clue to the answer can be found in the New Testament itself—in Paul's letter to the Galatians. In chapter four, he describes what it means to be a son of God. He begins with an example taken from everyone's daily experience. "I mean that the heir, as long as he is a child, is no better than a slave, though he is the owner of all the estate; but he is under guardians and trustees until the date set by the father" (Gal 4:1-2).

Paul takes for granted an idea that would have been instinctively obvious to all his hearers—that a child, even the heir of the estate, has a very lowly position in the household ("no better than a slave").

Children in Israel at the time of Jesus were at the low end of the social totem pole. They had very

few privileges. They were not fussed over, were
not idealized, were not the center of adult atten-
tion. Rather, they were expected to be of service in
whatever way they could, to be at their parents'
disposal, and to be respectful and obedient.

The exalted position of "son of God" that the
New Testament describes in Galatians, Romans,
and elsewhere is not a description of a young
child's relationship with his father. A son did not
become fully a "son" until he reached adulthood
and entered a mature relationship with his father.
It is into this mature, adult relationship with the
Father that Christians have entered through Jesus
Christ, says Paul in Galatians, and so we are no
longer in the lowly position of children under the
tutelage of the law.

In his teaching on becoming like children,
then, Jesus is speaking directly to the disciples'
concern for position and greatness. His words
are paradoxical, reversing what his followers
would have expected. To be great, to hold a high
position involves putting oneself at the disposal
and service of all. A disciple, says Jesus, should
not seek personal honor and glory. He should
not strive for the praise and adulation of men.
Neither should he aim to enhance his own
power, position, or reputation. Instead he should
take a child's position—humbly serving others
before serving himself.

This simple passage, so often misunderstood,
contains vital instruction for anyone seeking to be
a true follower of the Lord Jesus. It is a strong and

Prov. 17:6

consistent element in Jesus' instruction to his disciples. Matthew 18 is not the only passage where his paradoxical teaching on the greatness of the kingdom of heaven appears. Indeed, as we shall see, Jesus himself places this message at the very heart of his mission to the world.

"Not to Be Served, but to Serve"

One might think that Jesus' astonishing lesson on childlike lowliness would now be emblazoned upon the minds of the disciples. Yet it was a hard teaching—hard to understand and hard to put into practice—and it is not long before the disciples give evidence that they have not fully understood. We pick them up again only a short time later, now on the road to Jerusalem, prior to Jesus' final Passover with his disciples.

The disciples have taken to the road with very different expectations than has Jesus. Despite his efforts to prepare them for the dark days of his passion and death, Jesus' disciples have turned their faces toward Jerusalem with eagerness and anticipation. The long-awaited time has finally come, they think. Jesus, God's chosen Messiah, is about to march on Jerusalem and declare his kingdom. It is only a matter of days now and the kingdom will be established. Two of his fiery disciples, James and John, the sons of Zebedee (aptly renamed by Jesus "the sons of thunder"), decide that now is the time to make their move. They and their mother approach Jesus.

Then the mother of the sons of Zebedee came up to him, with her sons, and kneeling before him she asked him for something. And he said to her, "What do you want?" She said to him, "Command that these two sons of mine may sit, one at your right hand and one at your left, in your kingdom" (Mt 20:20-21).

The wife of Zebedee approaches Jesus with great respect, kneeling before him and paying him the homage due a king-to-be. She asks that he grant her only one request: the positions of highest honor in his kingdom for her two sons. She and her sons are not motivated by celestial visions of thrones in heaven, awaiting glory in the next life. Their eyes are fixed on the imminent coming of the kingdom of God, which will be proclaimed when Jesus the Messiah reaches Jerusalem and begins to establish his world rule. And in their mind's eye, they can see it all now: There they are, sitting on Jesus' right and left, his most powerful and trusted counsellors, James and John, the sons of thunder, Number One and Number Two in the glorious kingdom of the Messiah.

Jesus refuses to grant this request, saying that it is not his to decide. James' and John's bid for power and position has not gone unnoticed, however. The other ten disciples, themselves eager for such greatness in Jesus' coming kingdom, are hot with indignation. Who did James and John think they were, trying such a power play? Jesus, knowing all that is in their hearts, takes the opportunity to re-teach his lesson on greatness and lowliness, this time with a different twist.

> But Jesus called them to him and said, "You know that the rulers of the Gentiles lord it over them, and their great men exercise authority over them. It shall not be so among you; but whoever would be great among you must be your servant, and whoever would be first among you must be your slave; even as the Son of man came not to be served but to serve, and to give his life as a ransom for many" (Mt 20:25-28).

His words about children had been hard to take, but here was an even greater blow. The only set of people in a Jewish household who stood lower on the social ladder than the children were the servants (slaves). First Jesus had said that his disciples must be as lowly as children. Now he was going one better by insisting that their lowliness be as that of slaves.

What Is a Servant?

As with our notion of children, our modern Western notion of a servant can at times prevent us from catching the full impact of Jesus' familiar words. Household servants or slaves are hardly an everyday reality in our society, particularly in the U.S. For some of us, the word "servant" calls to mind that upstanding individual in society commonly known as the "public servant."

Take Joe O'Brien, for instance. He's a talented,

well-educated big-hearted businessman, grateful for the opportunities and blessings he has received. One of his desires in life is to help his fellow man. Joe earns more than enough to maintain his family in their pleasant suburban home, and he tries to be generous with both his time and money. He donates to several charitable organizations and is a member of the local school board. He has helped to sponsor a cultural enrichment program in his city and is even considering running for City Council in the next election—putting in a few years of even higher dedication to public service.

Joe is doing his best to place himself in the position of a servant—a public servant. Such public service is a very respectable, even dignified position in which to be found. A public servant is well-appreciated by his beneficiaries, held up before all as an example, and graced with the satisfying and fulfilling experience of doing good for others. As commendable and satisfying as Joe's public service may be, it is a far cry from the lowly position of servant (that is, "slave") which Jesus demands. One can be a "public servant" without humbling (that is, lowering) oneself in the slightest. Joe O'Brien can be his own man, calling his own shots, choosing his own service, while being a fine public servant at the same time.

Doing Whatever the Master Wants

When Jesus speaks of being a servant, he is referring to something much more difficult, demanding, and total than the contemporary notion of a "public servant." He has in mind someone whose entire life is summed up in that single word, "servant." A brief look at his words in Luke 17 will make this fact clearer.

"Will any one of you, who has a servant plowing or keeping sheep, say to him when he has come in from the field, 'Come at once and sit down at table?' Will he not rather say to him, 'Prepare supper for me, and gird yourself and serve me, till I eat and drink; and afterward you shall eat and drink'? Does he thank the servant because he did what was commanded? So you also, when you have done all that is commanded you, say, 'We are unworthy servants; we have only done what was our duty' (Lk 17:7-10).

As he had done when talking about becoming like a child (Mt 18), Jesus borrows a common image from daily life to teach his disciples how to live in the kingdom of heaven. They are to take on the lowliness of servants. At the time of Jesus, servants had fewer rights and privileges than those who were free. Their lives were not their own but were oriented to the service of another— their master. Only after all of the master's needs were met could they turn to their own. Jesus' portrayal of a servant in Luke 17 shows us an individual with no other job description than "to do whatever the master commands." The servant can be told to plow, to tend the animals, to cook, to wait at table, to clean up, or anything else. If the master says, "Prepare my meal," the servant doesn't answer, "Sorry, boss, you got the wrong guy. All I do is plow fields." When the master requires service at the end of a long day, the servant doesn't say, "Hey, c'mon. I've already put in my eight hours. Ask me tomorrow." Nor does the servant expect to be touted and congratulated for all his labors. Jesus rhetorically asks, "Does a master thank his servant for obeying his commands?"—the obvious answer being: "Of course not!"

These are very difficult and trying words. Our inexperience with the kind of servanthood to which Jesus points can obscure just how hard a saying Jesus' teaching is, but to men like the disciples, who were more familiar with the life of a servant, the force of this teaching is inescapable.

A recent discussion increased my appreciation for the power and the challenge of these words of Jesus. A friend of mine was visiting from the Philippines, a country where, as in many Third World nations, a large number of upper- and middle-class people have servants. Several of us got into a discussion with him about the ideal of servanthood which Jesus presents, and we Americans began to speculate about the daily existence of a servant. My friend sighed and shook his head. "You guys in the U.S. can't fully understand how hard it is to do what Jesus is calling for. In our country, many people have servants. Sometimes the servants will live their whole lives in their masters' service—at times not marrying, having little personal life of their own. And the social gap between masters and servants is immense. Taking on the role and position of a servant is a very difficult lesson for our people to accept and to learn, especially those who are well-off, because they really know what it means."

Jesus: The Perfect Example

Jesus really knew what it meant, too. And he was in dead earnest that his disciples learn this vital lesson of kingdom life. But Jesus didn't just teach the lesson about becoming a servant; he lived it. Perhaps had we only received an account of his words, we might more justifiably hem and haw, complaining that the words are hard to understand, or that they mean something else— something easier and more comfortable. We can claim no such justification, though. We have the teaching of Jesus presented to us in human form, lived out in his own flesh and blood. Jesus himself is the perfect example, our surest model, of the lowliness and humility of a servant.

In him, we see the lesson of servanthood played out on the grandest scale imaginable. For in the fullness of time, the second person of the Trinity, the mighty Word of God, in whom and through whom and for whom all things were created, and under whose headship all things will be united, lowered himself and became flesh. He put aside all the splendor and glory of his position to take on the form of a slave (Phil 2:5-8). The degree to which Jesus lowered himself for our sake boggles the mind. As C. S. Lewis comments in *Mere Christianity*:

> The Eternal Being, who knows everything and who created the whole universe, became not only a man but (before that) a baby, and before that a foetus inside a Woman's body. If you want to get the hang of it, think how you would like to become a slug or a crab.[2]

Jesus came in fulfillment of God's promises to his people, promises such as those spoken through the prophet Isaiah. One strain of Isaiah's prophecy foretells the coming of the Servant of the Lord, "my chosen one with whom I am pleased" (Is 42:1), whose life would be given as an offering for sin for the salvation of his people. "Through his suffering, my servant shall justify many, and their guilt he shall bear" (Is 53:11). Throughout his earthly ministry Jesus was keenly aware of his identity, his mission as the Servant of the Lord—a mission that would be fulfilled most perfectly in his death and resurrection.

In instructing his disciples that they become as servants, he was not insisting that they follow some new and uncharted course. He was teaching them that as true disciples, they must do as he did, walking the same path that he walked before them. He makes this point very forcefully in Matthew 20:28. Having instructed them in the spiritual principle of being servants, he proceeds to point out that he is their standard of behavior. They are to become slaves, "even as the Son of man came not to be served but to serve, and to give his life as a ransom for many." Jesus, the glorious and exalted Son of man, who had every right to be honored, worshipped, and served, had come rather to serve. His service would extend to the point of "giving his life as a ransom for many"—probably an intentional echo of the prophecy of the suffering servant in Isaiah 53.

Jesus was careful to repeat this message once again, during his last instructions to his disciples before his death. To their surprise and chagrin, in the midst of the Last Supper Jesus humbled himself as a servant before the Twelve, stooping to wash their feet—a lowly task befitting only the lowest and most menial household servant. This he did for their instruction, saying, "I have given you an example, that you also should do as I have done to you" (Jn 13:15). Surely, Jesus considers this lesson to be of central importance for his disciples, reinforcing it at his last opportunity before parting from them.

A Formidable Task

It is very striking how strongly and insistently Jesus returns to these ideas during the last days of his earthly life. He seems very concerned that his disciples learn childlike and servant-like lowliness. They are to see it in him, and they are to live it out in their own lives. The instruction and example that Jesus gives are not simply for his original disciples. They are of the utmost importance for all who would follow him, in any place, in any age.

As Jesus' disciples, we also must learn to take on the role and position of a servant.

It should not surprise us to find that taking on the full identity of "servant" is a formidable task, that we recoil at the prospect of not belonging to ourselves. Nor should it shock us that we must contend with selfish ambition, the desire for glory, position, and power. After all, were not these among the very temptations with which Satan tried to lure Jesus away from his true mission?

> Again, the devil took him to a very high mountain, and showed him all the kingdoms of the world and the glory of them; and he said to him, "All these I will give you, if you will fall down and worship me" (Mt 4:8-9).

And were they not also some of the temptations which worked most strongly on the Twelve, the men who knew Jesus better than anyone, who had travelled and lived with him constantly for almost three years, who had heard his teaching and seen his life: how he spoke, how he acted, how he bore himself? Even these closest of disciples, at the end of three years together, were still capable of strong selfish ambition, still vulnerable to the lure of glory and position.

We should not be alarmed to find the same fight going on in us. Ever and again, Satan has offered God's people a different way, easier and more attractive than the hard and painful way of the imitation of Christ. The seductive voice of the serpent, the alluring promises of the world around us, the driving force of our flesh within us would conspire to lead us down the wide and easy path of self-seeking. But the grace of God our Father, the teaching and example of Jesus, and the power of the Holy Spirit within us will enable us to conquer and to follow in the footsteps of our Master, down the narrow and difficult path of the servants of the Lord.

"Humble yourself like a child." "Become a servant." Herein lies the paradoxical greatness of the kingdom. The high road to heaven, says Jesus, is taken by the humble and lowly of heart. It is on this road that we press on towards true greatness, laying down our lives for God and his people as Jesus and his faithful followers have done before us. It is on this road of lowliness and humility that we set our sights on the final, ultimate test of greatness, where before the throne of God we will hear our Master say, "Well done, good and faithful servant. Enter into the joy of your Master."

THREE

Meekness:
The Preeminent Quality
of a Servant

This high and noble quality of Christlike lowliness and servanthood is perhaps best summed up in the term "meekness." While there are some other aspects and elements of Christian servanthood (such as zeal, for instance), meekness—along with its intimately related partner, humility—is the preeminent quality of a godly servant. Yet this statement still leaves much to be said, for we have not yet defined meekness, nor have we described what it looks like. This is the task of the present chapter, and we will begin with a look at the linguistic background of the word.

What's in a Word?

In discussing the quality of meekness, we run up against some unexpected linguistic complications. A brief look at the Hebrew, Greek, and English terms will tell us why. In the Old Testament, the Hebrew word *anav/anavah* is used in two different but related ways. On the one hand, it describes an objective position of lowliness, the condition of being in a lower, disadvantaged class. (See Is 61:1; Ps 9:12 and 10:2). On the other hand, it describes a character trait, an attitude of mind and heart that a person takes on regardless of his or her objective status in life. (See, for instance, Nm 12:3, Prv 15:33, Zep 2:3).

In the New Testament, these different senses of the Hebrew are translated into two different Greek words. One of those words, *tapeinophrosune*, tends to be translated into English as "humility." This is the term that especially captures the more objective condition of lowliness. The other Greek word, *prautes*, describes the attitude of mind and is often translated by the English word "meekness."[3]

Humility and meekness are closely related all through the New Testament, expressing two aspects of the same basic reality—that servant-like quality which is so highly regarded and highly recommended for Christians. Jesus himself tells us that he is "meek and humble of heart" (Mt 11:29), and as the master is, so must be his disciples.

It is in discussing this Christian quality in English that we run into complications. The traditional word "meekness" is not in frequent use in modern English. As a result, many people have no clear idea of what it means. What is more, those who do have some notion of its meaning usually have in mind a collection of unpleasant and unattractive images which bear no relation to the behavior and character of Jesus.

Distorted Images of Meekness

For me, the term conjured up the spectre of Marvin Milksop, a timid, weak-kneed, insecure mouse of a fellow who is constantly being walked on by everyone in his life. Marvin is a man who can't say no. His kids run all over him, his wife dictates his life, and he lives in mortal dread of his boss. "Yes, dear. Whatever you say." "Yes, sir. All right, sir." Such words run like a constant refrain through the day, because Marvin never speaks his mind, never stands up for what he believes. He always knuckles under in the face of conflict or confrontation.

If by meekness is meant such a weak and spineless response to life, it is difficult to imagine how one can be both a strong person and a properly meek Christian. Fortunately, Marvin Milksop bears practically no resemblance to the meekness of Christ. Indeed, what Marvin manifests is not strong Christian character but defective human character.

One can encounter a second distorted picture of meekness—a distinctively Christian distortion. Popular among some Christians today is a gooey, sentimental picture of Jesus. It could be called "the meek and mild Jesus." He is depicted as soft, gentle, and sensitive, always concerned to see that everyone feels loved and accepted just as they are, never one to judge, to be stern, or to raise his voice in anger. All these qualities are lumped under "meekness." But the "meek and mild Jesus" has little in common with the Jesus of the gospels. In fact, they would hardly recognize each other.

J.B. Phillips makes this comment on the description of Jesus as "meek and mild":

> Mild! What a word to use for a personality whose challenge and strange attractiveness nineteen centuries have by no means exhausted. Jesus Christ might well be called "meek," in the sense of being selfless and humble and utterly devoted to what He considered right, whatever the personal cost; but "mild," never!
>
> Yet it is this fatal combination of "meek and mild" which has been so often, and is even now, applied to Him. We can hardly be surprised if children feel fairly soon that they have outgrown the "tender Shepherd" and find their heroes elsewhere.
>
> But if the impression of a soft and sentimental Jesus has been made (supported, alas, all too often by sugary hymns and pretty religious pictures), the harm is not over when the adolescent rejects the soft and childish conceptions. There will probably linger at the back of his mind an idea that Christ and the Christian religion is a soft and sentimental thing which has nothing to do with the workaday world. For there is no doubt that this particular "inadequate god," the mild and soft and sentimental, still exists in many adults minds.[4]

When Jesus says that he is meek, he means something quite different from what a modern

American would likely understand by the term. This makes "meekness" a tricky word to work with. Unfortunately, the alternatives that most English translations recommend do not do the job either. Words like "courtesy," "respectfulness," "gentleness," and "lowliness" capture some aspect of the scriptural term, but they leave out other important elements. And those words, too, are prone to inaccurate and unfortunate interpretations, which are a far cry from the godly quality we seek.

The Meaning of Meekness

In the face of several imperfect alternatives, the attempt here will be to rehabilitate the traditional term "meekness." "Meekness" allows for a much broader scope of meaning than any of the other suggested alternatives, and the fact that it is an uncommon word makes it easier to clear up misconceptions and define the term properly.

The lack of any single English word that truly expresses the full scope of the scriptural term is probably some indication of how much the whole concept of "meekness" has fallen out of favor in our day. The language of a culture transmits the values and ways of thinking of its people. One simple word in the language of one culture can defy adequate translation into that of another culture (short of a full essay describing its various aspects and shades of meaning) because that second culture has no equivalent concept or way of thinking. This is precisely what we run into when trying to translate the New Testament term for "meekness" into today's English. As a result, it will take the rest of this chapter to do it justice.

The fact that meekness, as scripture uses it, contains a wealth of meanings should not obscure the fundamental simplicity of the idea. Put simply, meekness is the primary quality of one who acts in the manner of a servant. It has nothing to do with being weak, timid, or mild-mannered, but it has everything to do with that quality which we examined in the previous chapter, upon which Jesus insisted so earnestly in Matthew 18 and 20. Being meek does not necessarily involve *feeling* like a servant, nor does it mean *enjoying* being a servant. The emphasis, rather, is on our attitude and behavior. What is required is that we actually get down to the business of serving.

Taking on the mind and behavior of a servant isn't merely one simple operation, however. The quality of meekness has numerous aspects, which we can identify in the Old and New Testaments.

Meekness Is Courtesy and Respect

One hallmark of a true servant is a gracious courtesy and respect which acknowledges and expresses the value and worth of others. This sort of courtesy is part and parcel of placing ourselves before others in a posture of service. An excellent example of this aspect of meekness is Abraham, "our father in faith." Genesis 18 recounts the episode of the Lord's appearance to Abraham in the visit of the three men.

And the Lord appeared to him by the oaks of Mamre, as he sat at the door of his tent in the heat of the day. He lifted up his eyes and looked, and behold, three men stood in front of him. When he saw them, he ran from the tent door to meet them, and bowed himself to the earth, and said, "My lord, if I have found favor in your sight, do not pass by your servant. Let a little water be brought, and wash your feet, and rest yourselves under the tree, while I fetch a morsel of bread, that you may refresh yourselves, and after that you may pass on—since you have come to your servant." So they said, "Do as you have said." And Abraham hastened into the tent to Sarah, and said, "Make ready quickly three measures of fine meal, knead it, and make cakes." And Abraham ran to the herd, and took a calf, tender and good, and gave it to the servant, who hastened to prepare it. Then he took curds, and milk, and the calf which he had prepared, and set it before them; and he stood by them under the tree while they ate (Gn 18:1-8).

Here we find Abraham, venerable and prosperous, resting by his tent in the hottest part of the day. Suddenly, he notices that three travellers have approached. They are complete strangers, and he an aged and respected man, yet he springs immediately into action, bowing and speaking to them as a humble servant, offering them the finest hospitality of his house, and waiting upon them himself. His courteous and respectful service is richly rewarded, for it turns out that these men were no mortals, but the messengers of the living God. (See Heb 13:2).

Who is to receive this courteous expression of meekness from us? It is surely not limited to those we know and love, for Abraham behaved in this way toward perfect strangers. The scriptures indicate that such courtesy and respect have an immensely wide scope. Titus 3:2 directs Christians "to speak evil of no one, to avoid quarreling, to be gentle, and to show perfect courtesy [literally, "meekness"] toward all men." "Toward all men." It would be difficult to suggest a broader range of application than that!

The book of Sirach in the Jewish wisdom literature emphasizes how universally we are to be courteously meek: "To the poor man lend an ear, and return his greeting courteously" [literally, "meekly"] (Sir 4:8). The point here is that the courtesy which springs from godly meekness is not reserved for the eminent and the respectable, but is extended (even especially) to those in a lowly position. Christian meekness, then, will manifest itself in the respectful courtesy we show not only to the highly-placed and important, but to the poor, the underprivileged, and all who are bereft of worldly honor.

Since the time of the early church, the story of St. Martin of Tours has been an example to Christians of this quality in action, and of God's pleasure in those who practice it. Martin was a young soldier in the Roman army in the fourth century A.D. who cut a dashing figure riding through the city streets in his fine uniform. One bitter winter's day as he rode through the city of Amiens in France he came upon a poor man standing half-naked and shivering in the road. Moved with compassion and Christian love, Martin leapt from his horse and pulled off the heavy cloak that he wore as protection against the piercing cold. Drawing his sword, he cut the cloak in half, humbly offering one piece to the poor man, and making do himself with the other half—a move which made him look ridiculous to others as he rode through the town. That night as he slept, however, he had a vision of the Lord Jesus standing before him in the poor man's clothes, wrapped in half of Martin's cloak and thanking him for his compassion and generosity.

This courteous respect, which should typify the Christian, is the complete opposite of the arrogance that characterizes so many of today's "heroes" and "superstars"—a self-centered disrespect and scorn that asserts itself at the expense of others. Take Alex Sanford, for example. At first glance he's a pretty impressive fellow. He is good looking, outgoing, witty, intelligent, and an accomplished surgeon. Even so, he has some glaring social defects. Alex is a man who shows no partiality toward anyone. Unfortunately, in his case this means that he demonstrates little or no respect for anyone but himself. He is either condescending or contemptuous and abusive toward everyone in his life: his wife, his children, his colleagues, his nurses. He is quick to criticize, to deride, to put down.

Now Susan James is a bit more selective in her arrogance. To certain people—especially the highly placed, the wealthy, and the renowned, she is the picture of respectful behavior, even fawning flattery. But to those who cannot make her "VIP" list, especially those who are clearly "beneath" her, a very different Susan appears—haughty, snobbish, and unwilling to offer others the time of the day.

Arrogance can appear in different people under different guises. One of its forms is scornful, challenging, hostile, and insulting. It is very expressive and demonstrative, and we could suitably describe it as "hot" arrogance. We can see it in all its heat in a man like Goliath, the Philistine champion who dared to challenge the armies of the living God.

> And there came out from the camp of the Philistines a champion named Goliath, of Gath, whose height was six cubits and a span. He had a helmet of bronze on his head, and he was armed with a coat of mail, and the weight of the coat was five thousand shekels of bronze. And he had greaves of bronze upon his legs, and a javelin of bronze slung between his shoulders. And the shaft of his spear was like a weaver's beam, and his spear's head weighed six hundred shekels of iron; and his shield-bearer went before him. He stood and shouted to the ranks of Israel, "Why have you come out to draw up for battle? Am I not a Philistine, and are you not servants of Saul? Choose a man for yourselves, and let him come down to me. If he is able to

fight with me and kill me, then we will be your servants; but if I prevail against him and kill him, then you shall be our servants and serve us." And the Philistine said, "I defy the ranks of Israel this day; give me a man, that we may fight together." When Saul and all Israel heard these words of the Philistine, they were dismayed and greatly afraid.

Although much of it is for show, a similar kind of "hot" arrogance could be said to characterize the antics of the great boxer, Muhammed Ali, whose pre-fight and post-fight songs, poems, threats, and claims ("I am the greatest!") combine with his taunts and jibes during a match to present a picture of brash, scornful insolence. Ali, however, performs much of his shenanigans in fun, and as a playful clown and a superb boxer he endears himself to many. Sadly, the majority of those who exhibit hot arrogance take themselves all too seriously.

There is a second, more subtle form of arrogance that has come into vogue recently, especially among young men. In fact, it can sometimes be subtle enough to escape detection as arrogance. In contrast to the "hot" variety described above, we might call this form "cool" arrogance. "Cool" arrogance is passionless and unexpressive. Rather than hurling insults and challenges, it smugly ignores others, displaying utter disinterest and a universal "that's cool" attitude. Its spirit is nicely caught and humorously satirized by Charles Schultz's portrayal of Snoopy as "Joe Cool" in the popular "Peanuts" comic strip—complete with sunglasses and a self-centered, style-conscious aloofness. This form of arrogance has been idealized and incarnated in a wide range of recent movie and TV "heroes," all of whom are woefully lacking in Christian character. At root, the contemporary ideal of "being cool" carries with it much that is arrogant, disrespectful, rebellious, and self-centered—the very opposite of the courteous, respectful, servant-like nature of Christ.

Meekness Means Forbearing

Courteous respect is only one facet of meekness. Another aspect strongly emphasized in scripture is the quality of forbearance: trustful patience in the face of abuse or suffering. To observe this quality in action, let us again turn to one of the great figures of the Old Testament—this time to Moses.

The Book of Numbers, chapter 12, opens with a description of a conflict. By this point in poor Moses' experience, conflict was becoming a fact of life. Much of his time since the triumphant night of the Passover in Egypt had been occupied with handling the never-ending complaints, gripes, slander, and rebellion of the people of Israel. But this latest challenge was especially tough to take because it was coming from his own brother and sister—Aaron and Miriam—who had all along been his staunchest supporters. Moses had contracted a marriage that was not to their liking, and which provided an occasion for their expressing a growing jealousy of his special preeminence among the people of Israel.

Miriam and Aaron spoke against Moses because of the Cushite woman whom he had married, for he had married a Cushite woman; and they said, "Has the Lord indeed spoken only through Moses? Has he not spoken through us also?" And the Lord heard it (Nm 12:1-2).

In the face of this unexpected and unwarranted attack by members of his own family, Moses is described by the Old Testament as "meek." "Now the man Moses was very meek, more than all men that were on the face of the earth" (Nm 12:3). This description does not mean that Moses was weak or ineffectual as a leader. On the contrary, he had already proven himself to be strong and decisive when the circumstances required. In this context, being "meek" means that Moses did not retaliate in kind to the rebellion of his brother and sister. He did not speak against them, returning evil for evil, but he trusted in the vindication of God. And vindication was precisely what he got. The Lord's response to the quarrel is reminiscent of a father who interrupts a spat between his children to sort out right from wrong. In this case, Moses is fully in the right, and God's judgment against Moses' accusers is clear. In fact, Moses further demonstrates his meekness by immediately assuming the role of intercessor on behalf of his stricken sister.

Now Moses was called meeker "than all men

that were on the face of the earth," yet there came after him, in the person of Jesus, the perfect example of forbearance in suffering. The New Testament strongly emphasizes this quality of meekness in the Lord, insisting that his disciples must do likewise when they suffer abuse unjustly. One of the clearest passages on the subject is found in 1 Peter 2:20-25.

> For what credit is it, if when you do wrong and are beaten for it you take it patiently? But if when you do right and suffer for it you take it patiently, you have God's approval. For to this you have been called, because Christ also suffered for you, leaving an example, that you should follow in his steps. He committed no sin; no guile was found on his lips. When he was reviled, he did not revile in return; when he suffered, he did not threaten; but he trusted to him who judges justly. He himself bore our sins in his body on the tree, that we might die to sin and live to righteousness. By his wounds you have been healed. For you were straying like sheep, but have now returned to the Shepherd and Guardian of your souls.

Here we find Peter's considered analysis of Jesus' behavior at the time of his Passion. Part of Jesus' intention, Peter tells us, was to explicitly set an example, "that you should follow in his steps." And what were his steps? Jesus held fast to righteousness even in the face of the serious unrighteousness committed against him. His tendency was not the common human response of counter-hostility—giving evil for evil. And despite his true nature, and the greatness, glory, and power which awaited him, Jesus did not threaten his persecutors with gory details of what he could and would do to them for their unspeakable atrocity against the Son of God. Throughout his sufferings, he was in control of himself and his responses, trusting fully in his Father, who would judge justly and bring about the total vindication of his Son.

A brief look at two incidents from the gospel accounts can fill in more of the picture of this feature of Jesus' meekness in action. First, in Luke 23:34, Jesus, in the excruciating agony of the crucifixion, intercedes with his Father on behalf of his executioners—an incredible display of his godly forbearance in suffering: "And Jesus said, 'Father, forgive them; for they know not what they do.' And they cast lots to divide his garments."

Then, in the Gospel of John, Jesus demonstrates his meekness before the tribunal of Annas, the former high priest. He shows respect and composure throughout. Even when he receives an unjust blow, he does not strike back physically or verbally. Yet his meekness is not weak and timid, but strong and dignified, as he speaks directly and self-assuredly to his assailant.

The high priest then questioned Jesus about his disciples and his teaching. Jesus answered him, "I have spoken openly to the world; I have always taught in synagogues and in the temple, where all Jews come together; I have said nothing secretly. Why do you ask me? Ask those who have heard me, what I said to them; they know what I said." When he had said this, one of the officers standing by struck Jesus with his hand, saying, "Is that how you answer the high priest?" Jesus answered him, "If I have spoken wrongly, bear witness to the wrong; but if I have spoken rightly, why do you strike me? (Jn 18:19-23).

How do the examples of Moses and Jesus apply to our daily lives? It is obviously not a question of one's becoming a milksop, for in both of them, meekness clearly proceeds from personal strength, not from weakness. We can identify a few important occasions of abuse and conflict in which Christlike meekness is called for.

Do Not Return Evil for Evil

First, we should respond meekly in the face of attack or accusation that is directed against us personally. It is very important for us to know that this is the Christian response, because personal attacks are such a common feature of relationships at work, school, in the neighborhood, and in families. Sadly, the story is the same even in Christian churches and prayer groups. Gossip, slander, backbiting, jealousy, and resentment are rife wherever you go. In the normal course of human events a well-tested "law of human relations" often prevails: "For every hostile action

Rom. 12:17-21

there will be (at least) an equal and opposite hostile reaction." But this is not the way of Jesus, the way of the cross. In Christlike meekness we are not to return evil for evil, slander for slander, resentment for resentment.

Of course, this is not to say that we are to stand idly by as our name is trampled in the dust, or that we must passively refuse to defend ourselves when falsely accused. The meekness of Jesus allows for a dignified and reasonable self-defense— clearly stating the truth, dealing directly with lies or inaccuracies, and going personally to the hostile party to resolve the dispute. What we must *not* do is to respond in kind to personal attacks upon us. That is the way of the world, and Christians are not to follow it. It is, among other things, an immature, juvenile reaction. It reminds me of the fights we had as kids. One of us would toss out a nasty name, to be answered by a kick or a shove from the other, the initial attack quickly escalating into total war. God states the same thing we so often heard from our parents: "Yes, what your brother did was wrong. But two wrongs never make a right." We must not return wrong for wrong, but handle attacks upon us in the spirit of Jesus.

Enemies of the Gospel

Second, a meek response is called for in a Christian's disputes with enemies of the gospel. This is the instruction of Paul to Timothy in 2 Timothy 2:24-26.

Jude 9

And the Lord's servant must not be quarrelsome but kindly to every one, an apt teacher, forbearing, correcting his opponents with gentleness. God may perhaps grant that they will repent and come to know the truth, and they may escape from the snare of the devil, after being captured by him to do his will.

meekness a condition necessary for redeeming?

Again, Paul's directions on meekness illuminate the quality in action for us. The Lord's servant is to be kind and forbearing, and to avoid the vindictive quarreling and name-calling into which serious disagreement on important issues can degenerate. At the same time, the whole spirit of Paul's description points to meekness as the quality of the man who is in charge of the situation: confidently and generously, yet also forthrightly, stating the truth and correcting falsehood. His words can even be very strong and at times angry (as Jesus' words to the Pharisees in Matthew 23), but the Christian's desire to see enemies of the gospel "repent and come to know the truth" and "escape from the snare of the devil" will temper his response with the meekness that Paul enjoins.

Persecution

A third important occasion calling for meekly forbearance in the face of abuse is closely related to the second: we are to be meek when undergoing persecution for the sake of the gospel. The First Letter of Peter, which is addressed to Christians who seem to be facing the prospect of persecution, offers some of the strongest teaching in the New Testament on this subject. We have already observed the passage in chapter 2 on the forbearance of Christ. A bit later, in chapter 3, Peter takes up the question of suffering as a Christian.

> Do not return evil for evil or reviling for reviling; but on the contrary bless, for to this you have been called, that you may obtain a blessing. . . . Now who is there to harm you if you are zealous for what is right? But even if you do suffer for righteousness' sake, you will be blessed. Have no fear of them, nor be troubled, but in your hearts reverence Christ as Lord. Always be prepared to make a defense to any one who calls you to account for the hope that is in you, yet do it with gentleness [literally, "meekness"] and reverence (1 Pt 3:9, 13-15).

The New Testament offers more than instruction, however. It offers examples. In the Acts of the Apostles, for instance, we have the remarkable example of Stephen (Acts 7:54-60), as well as the consistent behavior of Paul and his companions (see Acts 14:19-20; Acts 16:22-34; Acts 22-26).

We encounter this godly meekness in the face of persecution and martyrdom in great Christian men and women from the time of the early church to our own day. Polycarp, the great second-century bishop and martyr, was ready to surrender his life immediately when persecution began in his city of Smyrna. Convinced by his friends to go into hiding, he was eventually betrayed and discovered by the authorities, who were seeking his death. His response when they arrived to arrest him was to welcome them graciously, to see to it that they received a good meal while he took some last hours to pray, and to go meekly (yet with strength and dignity) to his martyrdom in the arena. Fifteen centuries later, Jean de Brebeuf, a French Jesuit missionary in Canada, was undergoing the agonies of torture and death at the hands of the ferocious Iroquois Indians. His response was to lift up his eyes to pray, calling upon the name of Jesus, and to exhort his fellow Jesuit and the Indian Christians with him to faithfulness and endurance when their own turn to suffer and die would shortly come. In our own day, Richard Wurmbrand, an evangelical pastor from Rumania, submitted meekly and courageously to tremendous suffering at the hands of his communist persecutors. He lived to tell his story in *Tortured for Christ*.

We know about the love of Christ toward the communists by our own love toward them.

I have seen Christians in communist prisons with 50 pounds of chains on their feet, tortured with red-hot iron pokers, in whose throats spoonfuls of salt had been forced, being kept afterward without water, starving, whipped, suffering from cold, and praying with fervor for the communists. This is humanly inexplicable! It is the love of Christ, which was shed into our hearts. . . .

A minister was thrown into my cell. He was

half dead. Blood streamed from his face and body. He had been horribly beaten. We washed him. Some prisoners cursed the communists. Groaning, he said, "Please, don't curse them! Keep silent! I wish to pray for them."

A flower, if you bruise it under your feet, rewards you by giving you its perfume. Likewise Christians, tortured by the communists, rewarded their torturers by love. We brought many of our jailors to Christ. And we are dominated by one desire: to give communists who have made us suffer the best we have, the salvation which comes from our Lord Jesus Christ.[5]

With such clear instruction from scripture, the explicit example of Jesus, and so great a cloud of faithful witnesses down through the centuries, the call to meekness in the face of abuse and persecution becomes an inspiring call to courage, strength, and faithfulness in following the footsteps of the Master.

Meekness Means Being Teachable and Obedient

Obedience is another important quality of a good servant—an immediate responsiveness to direction or correction, a readiness to learn whatever might better serve the master. James points to this aspect of meekness in the first chapter of his letter.

Know this, my beloved brethren. Let every man be quick to hear, slow to speak, slow to anger, for the anger of man does not work the righteousness of God. Therefore put away all filthiness and rank growth of wickedness and receive with meekness the implanted word, which is able to save your souls (Jas 1:19-21).

A willingness to be taught, a readiness to obey—these are precious Christian qualities that are out of fashion in a society whose young people anxiously count the years until they will reach the magic age of eighteen, when no one can tell them what to do anymore. Yet in my experience of helping people to grow in the Christian life, I have learned to appreciate how vitally important is this quality of being teachable, if we are to advance in Christian maturity.

Take Jerry, for example. Jerry was a fellow who had a lot going for him. He was intelligent, gifted, personable, and well-liked. He was also sincerely interested in knowing and serving God. However, his background was only minimally Christian, and he had much to learn and understand. To his good fortune, Jerry had several friends and acquaintances around him who were both willing and able to instruct him and help him progress as a Christian. But, to his great misfortune, Jerry didn't seem to have a "teachable" bone in his body. He was stubborn and headstrong about his own opinions and highly resistent to receiving the help that was offered him. As a result, this young man who showed such promise and had so much going for him made very little progress as a Christian. In fact he made some big mistakes during the years that I knew him.

Our attitude should be that of the wise man who wears out the doorstep of one wiser than himself in the pursuit of wisdom (Sir 6:36). We should be ready, as servants of our God, to learn gladly from any who can teach us, without letting pride, embarrassment, or shame stand in our way.

Meekness and Authority

Being teachable and obedient particularly characterize the meekness of a subordinate. But those in a subordinate position are not the only ones who are called to meekness. As we saw in the previous chapter, Jesus speaks with great force in Matthew 20 about the servant-like posture which must characterize those who bear Christian authority. For a Christian, there is no "lording it over" others, no room for glory-seeking, no place for self-serving. Rather, a Christian leader is to express graciousness, courtesy, and esteem toward those he leads and cares for. Jesus' invitation in Matthew 11:28-30 runs precisely along these lines.

> Come to me, all who labor and are heavy laden, and I will give you rest. Take my yoke upon you, and learn from me, for I am gentle [literally, "meek"] and lowly in heart, and you will find rest for your souls. For my yoke is easy, and my burden is light.

Jesus speaks here from the position of a master, and his words invite disciples to come and follow him. The phrase "take my yoke upon you and learn from me" is another way of saying "enter into discipleship under me." Jesus then proceeds to describe himself with the very terms that epitomize the servant; he is "meek and lowly of heart"—once again the perfect example of his own teaching. In his exercise of authority, Jesus demonstrates how to differ from the "rulers of the Gentiles" by becoming a master who is a servant.

What does this servant-like exercise of authority look like? It would be quite possible to misapply the image in a very confusing manner and be left thinking that Jesus is instructing Christian leaders to take their directions from their subordinates. To clarify how the teaching of Jesus applies to a leader, let us use the analogy of a servant at a great banquet. The servant is called upon to serve the various diners in different ways. First of all, he serves the master of the house, watching him attentively, responding to his signals and directions. Second, he serves all the guests at table. His service to the guests, though, is different from his service to the master. He provides for the guests' needs and serves them the food *as the master directs*. The servant does not have twenty masters at table, but one. If one of the guests says, "Let's skip the soup and get right to the main meal," the servant looks to the master to get his orders, denying the guest's requests if the master so directs.

So it is with a Christian leader who is a servant. Who is his master? Surely, it is God from whom he takes his orders; it is God's will that he seeks to

learn and fulfill. And all the people that he serves
are served according to the Master's directions, not
merely according to their own preferences and
opinions. In this way, a leader can assume a servant's posture toward those he leads without abdi-
cating the spiritual authority he is called upon to
exercise.

Meekness, as we have seen, is a many-
splendored thing. It is more than courtesy, or
respect, or gentleness, or forbearance, or being
teachable. It includes them all. It is a quality for
young and old, men and women, leaders and
followers. It has its applications in good times and
in bad, towards one's closest friends and towards
one's enemies, as well as towards perfect
strangers. In the final analysis, it is a constellation
of qualities that characterize the true servant and
that are the essence of that childlike humility,
without which one will never enter the kingdom of
heaven.

→ ain't it the truth? the boozy man of the street
may demand, but he can't command. And etc.

FOUR

Christian Zeal:
The Other Side of the Coin

In order to fully understand the nature of meekness in Jesus' servant-like character, it is imperative that we see it in relation to his burning zeal for the kingdom of God. Jesus' zeal complements his meekness. Viewing both traits side by side in Christ's life helps to fill out the picture of servanthood in action. In the second chapter, we left Jesus and his disciples on the road to Jerusalem. Let us now pick them up again some days later as they near the Holy City. A little stage-setting will help us to understand the ensuing events.

It is the Sunday before Passover, the day that will always be remembered as Palm Sunday. Jesus has chosen this day for his triumphal entry into Jerusalem. His timing is no mere coincidence, for the season of Passover held special significance for the Jews. It was popularly believed that the Messiah would come at Passover time to announce the establishment of his kingdom. And many in Jerusalem and throughout Palestine were acquainted with the itinerant preacher from Galilee. There was much speculation and discussion concerning him: Who was he? Could he be the Messiah? Would he come to the feast? When would he make his move?

> Now the Passover of the Jews was at hand, and many went up from the country to Jerusalem before the Passover, to purify themselves. They were looking for Jesus and saying to one another as they stood in the temple, "What do you think? That he will not come to the feast?" (Jn 11:55-56).

Speculation had intensified recently because of the amazing reports coming from Bethany, a town just over the Mount of Olives to the east. Jesus had miraculously called his friend Lazarus back to life after he had been dead four days. Jerusalem was in a furor, buzzing with speculation over this latest sign, eager to see what Jesus would do when he arrived for Passover. When news came that Jesus had arrived in Bethany to spend the night with Lazarus and his sisters, it evoked an immediate response in Jerusalem. "When the great crowd of the Jews learned that he was there, they came, not only on account of Jesus but also to see Lazarus, whom he had raised from the dead" (Jn 12:9).

The following day, Jesus set out to make his entry into Jerusalem. At Bethphage, the next town after Bethany, he halted. The law required all pilgrims to stay in Jerusalem at Passover. But the city's normal population was around 50,000 and it couldn't accomodate the 100,000 pilgrims that flooded into it during Passover. Therefore, Jerusalem's outer limits were legally expanded, and Bethphage was included. At this point, then, before entering the village, Jesus prepared very deliberately for his entry into the city of Jerusalem. He had already made arrangements for a donkey to be provided, and then he sent two disciples ahead to procure it.

> And when they drew near to Jerusalem and came to Bethphage, to the Mount of Olives, then Jesus sent two disciples, saying to them, "Go into the village opposite you, and immediately you will find an ass tied, and a colt with her; untie them and bring them to me. If any one says anything to you, you shall say, 'The Lord has need of them,' and he will send them immediately" (Mt 21:1-3).

To our minds, entering the city on a donkey may seem insignificant, or perhaps even a bit degrading. But at that time in Jerusalem it was a dignified and stately arrival, fitting for a king.

Let us also recall the eager expectations brewing in the minds and hearts of Jesus' followers, as well as in the hearts of many devout Jews. The time is right. they think, the stage is set. *Now* will the kingdom of God be announced; *now* Jesus is marching triumphantly on Jerusalem, there to set up his royal throne. As Jesus enters the city, his own disciples and the crowd from Jerusalem go wild with exultation, greeting him with the royal title of son of David, proclaiming him King of Israel, and quoting from the messianic Psalm 118:

"Hosanna! Blessed is he who comes in the name of the Lord!"

Jesus then enters Jerusalem as the royal son of David. He is very explicit about his manner of entry, for he comes in great dignity, yet not with a vast army to capture the city. Without apology he presents himself to Jerusalem and the leaders of Israel as their King. He refuses to silence the joyful proclamations made by his disciples (see Lk 19:39-40), and yet his entrance is meek and not warlike. All of this is in fulfilment of the prophecy spoken of him by Zechariah (9:9), as Matthew notes: "Tell the daughter of Zion, Behold, your king is coming to you, humble [literally, "meek"] and mounted on an ass, and on a colt, the foal of an ass" (Mt 21:4-5).

In all these events, Jesus was declaring important truths about himself. Truly, he was the Christ, the son of David; yet he was not coming in the way the Jews had expected. He would not present himself as a conquering warrior-king, come to destroy the hated Roman Empire and to set up a temporal world-rule in Jerusalem. Rather, he had come as the meek and humble servant-king foretold by Zechariah—in a spirit of peace.

His very next action displays an important aspect of the nature of this meek and peaceful king—a bold and forceful zeal for his Father's house. Jesus enters the temple, the holiest place on the face of the earth, and aggressively drives out the money-changers and merchants who have set up shop in the outer court.

And Jesus entered the temple of God and drove out all who sold and bought in the temple, and he overturned the tables of the money-changers and the seats of those who sold pigeons. He said to them, "It is written, 'My house shall be called a house of prayer'; but you make it a den of robbers" (Mt 21:12-13).

John describes Jesus' cleansing of the temple as the fulfillment of the prophetic statement in Psalm 69: "Zeal for your house will consume me."

According to the New Testament Jesus manifested a strong and godly zeal in this aggressive act. He did not, as some people suggest, lose his cool, fly off the handle, or depart from his normal path of balanced, rational behavior. He was making no embarassing mistake in a fit of anger, which he would regret later, once he regained self-control. He knew exactly what he was doing, and he chose to act in precisely the manner in which he did. Throughout his ministry, Jesus was humble and meek at the proper time. And at the proper time he was authoritative, forceful, and aggressive. He was, at one and the same time, a man of meekness and a man of zeal.

What Is Zeal?

As with meekness, many people labor under an inaccurate or insufficient concept of zeal. A lot of Christians tend to equate zeal with enthusiasm. Though these two are related, they are different in many respects. Enthusiasm involves an eagerness or excitement that generally contains a large emotional component. As a result, it usually comes and goes in spurts. It is difficult to sustain a continual high level of enthusiasm without a lot of undue strain and weariness. Unfortunately, those who make the mistake of equating enthusiasm with zeal can feel bound to live at an unreasonable level of emotional intensity. Or else they can feel guilty and less than zealous for failing to maintain such a level.

I've known other Christians who have succeeded in making themselves somewhat obnoxious and difficult to relate to through their misguided efforts to be "zealous." In order to be a strong and zealous Christian, it is not necessary to wear a perpetual, "joyful," toothy grin, to speak in "pious-sounding" Christian jargon, or to unleash a heavy blast of high-intensity enthusiasm at everyone we encounter. In fact, it is not only unneccessary, but unadvisable and wearisome—for everyone involved.

In essence, true zeal consists of a determined, aggressive dedication to something or someone. It should not come and go in a Christian's life, because it is not subject to the vagaries of the more emotion-based enthusiasm. Christian zeal is a constant feature of a strong Christian life, because it is a dedication to God founded on a fundamental decision. It's not affected by how we're feeling, what day it is, how we slept last night, or whether things are going our way. It is certainly true that enthusiasm supports our zeal for God and his kingdom, making our determined, aggressive actions easier to sustain. But our zeal should last through thick and thin, long after enthusiasm has waxed and waned, and waxed and waned again.

In scripture, both the Hebrew word (*qinah*) and the Greek word (*zelos*) can be translated into English in two related ways: "zeal" and "jealousy." For example, in the Old Testament God's *qinah* is at times translated as God's zeal (Is 9:7—"The zeal of the Lord of hosts shall do this") and at other times as his jealousy (Ez 16:41-42—"I will make you stop playing the harlot, and you shall also give hire no more, so I will satisfy my fury on you, and my *jealousy* shall depart from you"). Furthermore, the scripture regards zeal as a potentially good or bad thing, depending on how it is used and where it is directed. For instance, Paul speaks of the Jewish opponents of Christianity as possessing a zeal which misses the mark.

> I bear them witness that they have a zeal for God, but it is not enlightened. For, being ignorant of the righteousness that comes from God, and seeking to establish their own, they did not submit to God's righteousness (Rom 10:2-3).

In our own day, we could certainly say that communists exhibit an impressive measure of zeal, which is seriously misdirected, thereby making them dangerous enemies of the gospel.

Examples of Godly Zeal

On the other hand, true godly zeal is an attribute of all the great heroes of the faith. We have already noted Jesus' example. Let us take a brief look at the zeal of a few other great men and women of God. Earlier we noted the "hot arrogance" of Goliath of Gath. His opponent on the field of battle, the youthful David, gives us a prime example of a man's zeal for God. Righteously angered by the boasts, threats, and blasphemies of the Philistine champion, who had dared to defy the Lord, David courageously confronted Goliath in the name of his God.

> Then David said to the Philistine, "You come to me with a sword and with a spear and with a javelin; but I come to you in the name of the Lord of hosts, the God of the armies of Israel, whom you have defied. This day the Lord will deliver you into my hand, and I will strike you down, and cut off your head; and I will give the dead bodies of the host of the Philistines this day to the birds of the air and to the wild beasts of the earth; that all the earth may know that there is a God in Israel, and that all this assembly may know that the Lord saves not with sword and spear; for the battle is the Lord's and he will give you into our hand."
>
> When the Philistine arose and came and drew near to meet David, David ran quickly toward the battle line to meet the Philistine. And David put his hand in his bag and took out a stone, and slung it, and struck the Philistine on his forehead; the stone sank into his forehead, and he fell on his face to the ground (1 Sam 17:45-49).

Centuries later, in the face of another blasphemer, the burning zeal of Mattathias the priest and his five sons inspired Israel to resist their Syrian persecutor and to stand fast in their loyalty to God.

Then the king's officers who were enforcing the apostasy came to the city of Modein to make them offer sacrifice. Many from Israel came to them; and Mattathias and his sons were assembled. Then the king's officers spoke to Mattathias as follows: "You are a leader, honored and great in this city, and supported by sons and brothers. Now be the first to come and do what the king commands, as all the Gentiles and the men of Judah and those that are left in Jerusalem have done. Then you and your sons will be numbered among the friends of the king, and you and your sons will be honored with silver and gold and many gifts."

But Mattathias answered and said in a loud voice: "Even if all the nations that live under the rule of the king obey him, and have chosen to do his commandments, departing each one from the religion of his fathers, yet I and my sons and my brothers will live by the covenant of our fathers. Far be it from us to desert the law and the ordinances. We will not obey the king's words by turning aside from our religion to the right hand or to the left."

When he had finished speaking these words, a Jew came forward in the sight of all to offer sacrifice upon the altar in Modein, according to the king's command. When Mattathias saw it, he burned with zeal and his heart was stirred.

He gave vent to righteous anger; he ran and killed him upon the altar. At the same time he killed the king's officer who was forcing them to sacrifice, and he tore down the altar. Thus he burned with zeal for the law, as Phinehas did against Zimri the son of Salu (1 Mac 2:15-26).

Burning zeal is not an attribute solely of the men who served and fought for God. The same zealous spirit is to be seen in Deborah, who roused the faltering Barak into action to defeat the enemies of Israel (Jgs 4:4-10), and Judith, whose zeal for God and her people led her to courageous action and a single-handed victory over Israel's Assyrian persecutor (Jd 8-13).

One of the greatest examples of godly zeal is the apostle Paul. From his early years, Paul was a man of great zeal, as he himself describes in Galatians 1:13-14:

For you have heard of my former life in Judaism, how I persecuted the church of God violently and tried to destroy it; and I advanced in Judaism beyond many of my own age among my people, so extremely zealous was I for the traditions of my fathers.

Yet this zeal for the law, for the "traditions of his fathers," for God, was unenlightened as was that of many of his compatriots. For a time it led him to zealously persecute Christians. When he was struck from his horse on the Damascus road, the course of Paul's life was radically changed. But his zeal for God flamed on—now not only burning hotly, but enlightened by the light of Christ.

For the remainder of his life, Paul's consuming zeal for God would lead him on, constantly and unfalteringly. It was no smooth, easy path he walked, but one frought with toil and trouble, with untold hardship and grief. Paul himself tells us how rough things were for him:

> Are they servants of Christ? I am a better one—I am talking like a madman—with far greater labors, far more imprisonments, with countless beatings, and often near death. Five times I have received at the hands of the Jews the forty lashes less one. Three times I have been beaten with rods; once I was stoned. Three times I have been shipwrecked; a night and a day I have been adrift at sea; on frequent journeys, in danger from rivers, danger from robbers, danger from my own people, danger from Gentiles, danger in the city, danger in the wilderness, danger at sea, danger from false brethren; in toil and hardship through many a sleepless night, in hunger and thirst, often without food, in cold and exposure (2 Cor 11:23-27).

Here is a man motivated by more than mere enthusiasm. Paul's was a relentless, determined dedication of himself to God, which withstood unwaveringly all the ups and downs, the victories and defeats of the life God assigned to him.

How Do We Express Zeal?

Like meekness, zeal is a characteristic of a loyal and true servant. A faithful vassal in the service of a great king will be zealous for the king's honor and glory, and for the accomplishment of his plans and wishes. So it is with us and our great King. Our Christian zeal can and should find concrete expression in daily life. Scripture gives us pointers concerning where and how this zeal might be displayed. Let us look briefly at several of them.

Zeal for God Himself

Paul tells the Jews of Jerusalem in Acts 22:3 that from his youth he has been "zealous for God." For a Jew, this zeal would be especially focused on God's law, that gracious and priceless gift given to Israel on Mount Sinai. Zeal for God includes much more, however. In our daily lives, it involves our dedication to grow in the knowledge and love of God, to draw near to him regularly in prayer, to seek out and do his will, and to bring him glory by the way we live. In all of these things, enthusiasm and desire can play a useful part, but it is especially our zeal for God, our consistent and determined dedication to him, that will see us through—faithful to the end. Here is the starting point for zeal. Before expressing it in other ways, let us be sure that our zeal, first and foremost, is for God himself.

Zeal for the Gospel

We have already noted the zeal of Jesus and Paul in this regard. In the New Testament, Paul also uses the term explicitly in reference to one of his fellow workers, Epaphras: "For I bear him witness that he has worked hard for you [literally, "that he has great zeal for you"] and for those in Laodicea and in Hierapolis (Col 4:13).

Zeal in spreading the gospel of Christ has always characterized the church's apostolic workers and missionaries, from New Testament times to the present. For instance, in the early days of America, the Methodist circuit riders displayed remarkable zeal in their preaching of the gospel. These men often chose to remain single for the sake of their service to God, enduring such tremendous hardship and deprivation on their preaching circuits through the American wilderness that they seldom lived to be middle-aged. Their sacrificial dedication typifies the zeal of Christian missionaries down through the centuries. While most of us may not be called to such radical expression of zeal for the gospel, our dedication to aid in communicating the truths of our faith to those who do not know them is a normal expression of Christian zeal. It may take the form of financially supporting those who are called to be missionaries or of extending Christian love to people at work, in our neighborhood, or in the classroom. Much of my own work with university students concerns bringing the life of Christ to young men and women who do not have it or who have lost it. Time and again the uncomplicated love of a Christian friend, reaching out in word and action, has been the key to the conversion of such a student. Many of my Christian friends have been instrumental, at work or in their neighborhoods, in bringing others to faith—not through eloquent preaching but through consistent Christian love and the sharing of a single truth at the right time. "Normal" Christians can have a tremendous impact on friends and acquaintances when their zeal is channelled in this direction.

Zeal for Good Works

Paul writes to Titus that Jesus "gave himself for us to redeem us from all iniquity and to purify for himself a people of his own who are zealous for good deeds" (Ti 2:14). What kind of good deeds should we be zealous for? The range is very broad. It involves being of service "to all men, and especially to those who are of the household of faith" (Gal 6:10). In 1 Timothy 5:10, Paul describes the following good deeds of a godly widow: "one who has brought up children, shown hospitality, washed the feet of the saints, relieved the afflicted, and devoted herself to doing good in every way." Giving generously to supply the needs of others is another important good deed. Paul commends the church in Corinth (2 Cor 9:2) for its zeal in collecting money to go to the aid of the church in Jerusalem, which was in great need.

Like the New Testament Christians, we should be zealous for every good work: generous with our time, energy, goods, and money, not so that we can feel good about ourselves or so that others will think we're wonderful, but so that we will please God and obey his commandments. A zeal for good works is not the special property of certain unusual Christians; it is not outside the scope of a normal Christian life. I can point to many Christian families that have successfully integrated this willing generosity into a very busy schedule.

For instance, one friend of mine, a prosperous Christian businessman, has raised a fine family, shown gracious hospitality in his home, had a marked impact on the lives of many around him, and given freely of his time and money to Christian work, while effectively heading his own business. His demanding daily routine has in no way extinguished his zeal for good works.

Zeal in Defense of the Faith

Zeal in defense of the faith—of righteousness and truth—has characterized God's people since the first days of their covenant relationship with him. In Exodus 32:25-29, just after Moses descended from the mountain with the tablets of stone, the zeal of the sons of Levi broke out upon those worshipping the golden calf, cutting off idolatry—perhaps the greatest threat to the faith of Israel. Later, when idolatry, this time to the Baal of Peor, again threatened Israel, the zeal of Aaron's grandson Phinehas in punishing the guilty won him God's favor and averted the plague which was sweeping through the people due to

God's wrath (Nm 25:6-13). David's zeal in his
battle with Goliath and the zeal of Mattathias and
his sons—examples noted earlier—were expressions of godly zeal in defense of the faith, too. This
type of zeal is carried over into the New Testament—in Jesus himself, then in Peter, John, Paul,
Stephen, and others. It should characterize us,
also. As Peter says: "Always be prepared to make
a defense to any one who calls you to account for
the hope that is in you" (1 Pt 3:15). As we noted
earlier, this defense of the faith, zealous as it is,
must also be blended with meekness, if we are to
act in the spirit of the Lord. But true meekness will
not prevent us from taking a firm stand for the
truth and against wrongdoing. It will not keep us
from speaking out in protest when the Christian
faith is mocked and derided. At times, such a
stand may be unappreciated and unwelcome, and
it may cost us—in popularity, position, or even
health and safety. Whatever the cost, it is a price
worth paying for so great a treasure as the truth of
Christ.

One friend of mind recently faced an occasion
for expressing his zeal for Christian righteousness.
His boss presented him with new profit-making
policies that clearly required dishonest and decep-
tive dealings with others. "We can't do this," said
my friend. "This is just plain wrong." His boss
warned him that failure to comply could cost him
his job. My friend's rejoinder was that some things
were more important to him than his job. As a
Christian, he would not be party to underhand
and unethical business dealings. Because my

friend was such a good manager his boss decided to reverse the new policies in order to keep him. Many times, however, taking a stand for the truth is a much more expensive proposition. Christian zeal counts the cost and takes the stand.

As was true of meekness, Christian zeal has many facets. While we have looked at several major ones, the possibilities have by no means been exhausted. However, we have seen enough to recognize that the quality of zeal, which scripture so often attributes to God, is essential equipment for those who would be like him. While zeal may not epitomize the character of a servant as thoroughly as does meekness, it is vital to the full expression of servanthood in the Christian life. It adds an important dimension to our characters, one that is so apparent in the life of Jesus. Our aim should be that the words of Psalm 69 will apply to us as they did to Jesus himself: "Zeal for your house will consume me."

FIVE

Brokenness:
Taming a Christian's
Strength

The high call to be servants in the likeness of Jesus is made all the higher by the fact that few of us naturally desire to be servants. Indeed, ever since the Fall, we humans have been a stiff-necked, headstrong, rebellious, self-centered lot. And many of us have been shaped by the same forces that Paul describes to the Gentile Christians in Ephesus. We were "following the course of this world, following the prince of the power of the air," and "following the desires of body and mind, and so we were by nature children of wrath like the rest of mankind" (Eph 2:2-3).

To fully put on Christian meekness and zeal requires from us substantial internal change, because these servant-like, godly qualities wage war on the stiff-necked self-will and rebelliousness of our fallen nature. True meekness and zeal cannot be acquired simply by accepting the abstract theory. There must be a change within us, a death to ourselves. Some Christians have used the word "brokenness" to describe this necessary change. Rightly understood, I believe this idea can be of great use to us as we learn the meekness and zeal of Christ.

What Is Brokenness?

At least two very different images could come to mind when this term is used. One of them is somewhat inaccurate and unappealing. The other can be a very valuable aid to us. One misleading image of brokenness interprets it as a condition that involves being crushed or smashed. According to it we are something like the porcelain figurine my family had on one of our basement shelves. One night when we were kids, a violent thunderstorm knocked out the electricity supply to our house. A few of us were playing together in the basement when everything went pitch black. After a few moments of consternation and confusion, I said "Okay, everybody get in single file and hold on to the one ahead of you, and we'll all feel our way upstairs." I led the way, groping ahead of me in the dark. Unfortunately, the first thing I made contact with was that porcelain figurine. I drew my hand back quickly, but too late. It crashed to the floor and broke in several pieces. Even though we tried to glue it together, it was never the same. Something like this may happen to people who have come through the harrowing experience of brainwashing and torture. They can come out "broken men," who are never quite the same. Their spirit is crushed; they have no heart left to fight, or sometimes even to live.

This image has also been used of one who suffers a crushing personal defeat or humiliation. For example, in 1938 Adolf Hitler took over Czechoslovakia. Hitler accomplished this feat without a fight by summoning Czechoslovakia's president, Dr. Hácha, to Berlin. There, the Czech president, an old man in ill health, was kept up most of the night, mercilessly browbeaten by Hitler and his aides, and threatened with the destruction of his people. Finally, in despair, he consented to sign a statement that authorized the entry of Hitler's troops into Czechoslovakia. Hácha left Berlin defeated and utterly humiliated, a "broken" man.

Now, this idea of "brokenness" does not convey what God wants to do in changing us. He does not wish to crush us, to leave us in a weak, decrepit, or miserable condition. How could we be strong, forceful, and confident in serving him if that were the case? We would appear defeated rather than victorious.

The second and more accurate image of brokenness is really quite different. I can best depict it by describing a movie I saw many years ago. It was the story of a young Indian boy and a great, white, wild stallion. This horse was well known to the Indians of the territory, but no one had succeeded in catching, much less riding, this magnificent animal. The young Indian went out into the wilderness, and with great patience, love, and firmness succeeded in catching and then training the proud, wild beast to the point that it obeyed him, carried him bareback, and stood loyally with him to the death.

This is a good analogy for the kind of broken-ness that applies to us. The Lord is certainly not much like the Indian boy, but we are a quite a bit like that wild horse, whom the Lord must corral and then "break" with love, patience, and firm discipline. This notion of "breaking" a horse is frequently used by cowboys, not in reference to crushing a horse's spirit, but in regard to taming his wildness and curbing his will so that all his strength and ability can be harnessed and made useful.

Herein lies a key to both meekness and zeal. Our strength must be tamed and channelled by God if we are to be his profitable servants. While he loves us even in our wild, untamed condition, we will only be of limited use to him until he has "broken" and trained us. Once broken, we go from being headstrong, willful, selfish, and unpredictable to being responsive, obedient, and trustworthy ser-vants of God. There is no diminishing of strength entailed in being broken. If anything, our strength increases as we submit ourselves to God's training, because it is properly channelled and harnessed.

Breaking Self-Will

A fundamental internal change—this is what brokenness is all about. Part of this change in-volves letting go of our stubborn willfulness and our determination to get our own way. This letting go should characterize our thinking about major decisions we must make (eg., "What should I do with my life?" "Should I take that new job?" "Should we move or stay where we are?"). We must be free to do God's will, which sometimes coincides with our will but sometimes does not. This attitude should also characterize our approach to the small issues of our daily life, where our tendency is to push for getting our own way, even when it matters very little. We would do well when there is nothing more at stake than our own preferences to insist less often on what we want, and to let others have their preferences more frequently. This is especially true in marriage, where both husband and wife must undergo a certain breaking of their preferences and self-will.

For some of us, our problem with self-will is not immediately obvious, since it only surfaces on certain occasions. It tends to rear its head precisely at those times when we are crossed, when things don't go the way we want them to, or when others find fault with us. For instance, one women I know (we'll call her Sandra) is a very nice, kind person. She's generous and agreeable. But when Sandra wants something, she *wants* it. And she doesn't graciously take no for an answer, even from those who have authority to decide. At first resistance she prods and cajoles, but if the no remains no, her eyes begin to flash, her voice gets sharp, and she can become pushy and even nasty.

Or take my friend Bob. He's a very talented and likable fellow, who makes a good first impression. Bob is a firm believer, however, in the infallibility of his own opinion, and in the vast superiority of his way of doing something over all comers.

Awhile back, Bob, who teaches catechism in his Catholic parish, was corrected by the director of his program for taking a different approach to the material than the one they had agreed upon. Bob got irritated and defensive, tried several justifications of his methods, and showed great unwillingness to make the minor changes that his director required.

Sandra and Bob still have a lot to learn about Christian meekness. Some of that necessary internal breaking of self-will still needs to take place. Having their self-will broken, though, won't mean that they will become weak-willed or that they will lose all their capacity for having strong opinions or preferences. In fact, it is a great virtue to have a strong will, provided that it is exercised toward the proper ends. As Christians, we are to strongly exercise our wills toward the accomplishment of God's will. At the same time, we must learn to lay down our self-will: our attachment to our own way, our preferences, and our desires.

Breaking Wildness

The white stallion in the movie manifested his wildness by reacting violently whenever he was confronted with difficult circumstances. For example, if a man tried to approach him, he would react in fear, turn tail, and race off like the wind. When another stallion attempted to challenge his domain, he snorted and neighed with anger, pawed the ground, and charged in full fury with hoofs flying and teeth bared.

As with the horse, we can also have a streak of wildness that needs breaking—a tendency to violent emotional reactions when facing difficult situations: for instance, a tendency to freeze, or else to bolt and run in fear, or a tendency to lash out in anger. Being broken of our wildness means learning to overcome the unruly emotional reactions within us in such a way that we are free to make the response which is proper to a servant of the Most High King.

Being broken, even in the sense used in this chapter, is always a trying and painful experience. But there is no way around it for those of us who would take on the character of the Lord. Our strength must be brought under God's control, and our self-will and wildness must be broken in order to bring about the full internal change that frees us to be true servants of God.

SIX

The Gospel of Selfism

We have been looking thus far at a central feature of Christian character: following Jesus our Lord on the lowly path of Christian servanthood. We have seen that as true servants of the living God, we should manifest in our lives that blend of meekness and zeal found in Christ's own character. Taking on the Lord's character in this regard is no easy task. A key to making the necessary changes in us lies in brokenness—the taming and training of our strength to serve the purposes of God.

This Christian ideal of servanthood is truly a high and noble calling. It is not, however, the only ideal on the market. In our society it is diametrically opposed by the reigning secular ideal, which I will call "the gospel of selfism." In the next two chapters, we will compare the Christian ideal of character and its concrete expression with its modern secular counterpart. In this chapter we will compare the "gospel of selfism" to the ideal of servanthood. In the next chapter we will compare the Christian qualities of meekness and zeal with some prevailing patterns of behavior in our society today.

The Gospel of Selfism

A peculiar Western heresy, the gospel of selfism has met with surprising success in the twentieth century, considering its shallow, selfish goals and its myopic perspective on human life. In a relatively brief span of years it has worked massive changes in the ideas and attitudes of the man-on-the-street, without his conscious awareness or consent. In recent years, many sociologists and historians have been charting its progress, calling our time "the age of narcissism" and the "me generation."

The good news of the "me generation" is preached everywhere—at work and in the schools, in newspapers and magazines, radio and T.V., in the government and even at times in the churches. "Get ahead." "Be yourself." "Don't let anyone tell you what's right for you." "I'm okay, you're okay." "Fulfill yourself." "If it feels good do it." "Do your own thing." "Grab for all the gusto you can get." The catch phrases go on and on, proclaiming salvation through self-acceptance and self-fulfillment, reassuring us that all our personal desires merit satisfaction. As one ad puts it, "If you want it, you deserve it."

This new gospel was not concocted solely by the advertising agencies of our land, seeking to create a luxury-buying mentality in consumers. While the advertisers have certainly played their part, so have many others. Some of the foremost missionaries of this new "faith" are well-known social scientists (especially certain psychologists) and their popularizers.

Paul Vitz, a professor of psychology at New York University, has written an excellent Christian critique on some of the propagators of the "selfist" gospel, which he aptly entitles *Psychology As Religion: The Cult of Self-Worship*. According to Vitz, it is from the chairs of many university professors, from the offices of many psychological counsellors, and from bookstands offering the latest best-selling psychological self-help manuals that much of the strongest, most influential proclamation of the gospel of selfism comes to us.

The Gospel of Selfism and the Great Commandments

How does this strange, secular humanist faith match up with the gospel of Jesus? Very badly, to say the least. Before comparing it with Jesus' teaching on servanthood, let us look briefly at how it compares with Christ's two greatest commandments.

And one of the scribes came up and heard them disputing with one another, and seeing that he answered them well, asked him, "Which commandment is the first of all?" Jesus answered, "The first is, 'Hear, O Israel: The Lord our God, the Lord is one; and you shall love the Lord your God with all your heart, and with all your soul, and with all your mind, and with all your strength.' The second is this, 'You shall love your neighbor as yourself.' There is no other commandment greater than these" (Mk 12:28-31).

The love of God and the love of neighbor are of central importance in the Christian faith, but they have no place in the gospel of selfism.

In the "selfist" faith, God is not honored or worshipped as the one true God. In its purely secular forms, he is ignored or denied. In its Christian guise, he receives lip service, but little more. Paul Vitz's subtitle puts it very well. Selfism is a new religion, centered on worshipping the self. In selfism, then, we find people worshipping what must be the strangest of strange gods—themselves. For some, this self-idolatry is far from conscious, operating as a more subtle undercurrent in their philosophy of life. But for others, self-worship is boldly proclaimed as a way of life.

Vitz quotes one such example from a widely popular self-help movement. It is an extreme example, but it effectively captures much of the spirit of the selfist gospel.

You are the supreme being.

Reality is a reflection of your notions. Totally. Perfectly.

So you got the notion to play a little game with yourself. That is, you said to yourself something like, "Gee, this is rather boring. Wouldn't it be more FUN to COMMUNICATE." So you created a WORD game. That's all life is—one big word game. Don't lie to yourself about it anymore. They even wrote it down, not long after the beginning. They said, "AND THE WORD WAS GOD."

Of course it was.

Also notice that there isn't any right/wrong— it simply doesn't make SENSE to be unethical.

You had the notion that communicating would be more fun. And you created the rules. So you are responsible for the game as it is. All of it.

And it has no significance. You're IT. Choose. It has no significance. Choose. Life is one big "SO WHAT?" "CHOOSE."[6]

The opening line of this quote really says it all. In the purest forms of the gospel of selfism, there is no room for God. Man is the supreme being, and he lives in a strange world in which "reality" consists of whatever he prefers to believe. We are told to believe that we are the center of reality, and its judge. Everything is relative, and we can use our own subjective criteria to guide our beliefs. I have run into this idea many times while talking to people about Christianity. I recall talking with a university student once about Christian truth. After we had talked awhile he said, "Yeah, that's pretty interesting. But what I really think is . . . ," and he proceeded to lay out a confused hodge-podge of Western humanism, Eastern mysticism, and romantic back-to-nature ideas, some of which were not even internally consistent. "Now that's *very* interesting," I said. "But where did you come up with that?" "I thought it up myself," he told me proudly. "But," I asked, "what's your basis, your authority, for believing those things? What gives you any reason to suppose that any of those ideas are true?" "It's just the way I like to think about things," he stated defensively. "It's true for me."

For a Christian, certain truths are absolute. If God is, then he is. If Christianity is true, it is not just true for me because I like to think about things that way. It is simply true—for everyone. Those who subscribe to the gospel of selfism prefer to see all truth as relative. After all, as the passage quoted above states, we made up the rules of life in the first place, and we're free to change them. There is no one over us, no greater significance to life than what we choose to make of it. "Your own life," says the selfist, "is the whole show. Do what you want. Live for yourself. You're IT."

When put so baldly, these ideas sound patently absurd. Most reasonable people, especially Christians, don't buy them in their most blatant form. Rather, they quietly, even unconsciously, absorb more moderate versions of them from the selfist atmosphere around them. A set of underlying assumptions is formed that shapes their values and decisions in a selfish direction: "Your personal happiness and fulfillment are most important." "You can do what you feel like as long as you don't hurt anyone." "You are the one who decides what is right and wrong." These self-oriented assumptions seriously affect a Christian's relationship with God. They foster a very self-centered attitude toward him, consisting largely of "gimme, gimme, gimme." Such assumptions encourage the Christian to relate to God on the basis of "what I get out of it." They often leave Christians feeling quite at liberty to ignore God's commandments, provided that everyone is "sincere" and doesn't obviously hurt anyone else.

Selfist assumptions can also lead to a refusal to accept God as he has revealed himself. "I can't believe in a God who would throw people into hell" is an all-too-frequent refrain among some Christians, considering how clearly he has indicated his ability to do so when it is warranted. Insistence on a God who puts my personal fulfillment first, and who must meet all my requirements, is a sure sign that the gospel of selfism has penetrated a Christian's life.

So much, then, for love of God. The selfist gospel abolishes it or distorts it beyond recognition. Love of neighbor doesn't fare much better in the selfist gospel.

Following the teaching of the Old Testament (Lv 19:18), Jesus instructs his disciples to love their neighbors as themselves. This is not an exhortation on self-acceptance, as some people today tend to think. Jesus presumes that people generally take good care of themselves. He teaches them to take care of their neighbors as well. In Philippians 2:4, Paul says, "Let each of you look not only to his own interests, but also to the interests of others." Selfism reverses Paul's instructions and directs us to begin by "looking out for Number 1." Cover all your own needs and wants first. If there's anything left over, you can do good to others if you so choose. In its more extreme forms, it teaches a new golden rule: "Do unto others before they do unto you."

Selfism and the Family

This self-centered attitude is in evidence everywhere. It is prevalent even where it ought to be least expected: in the family. According to many sociologists, the American family is coming apart at the seams. The divorce statistics are staggering: by 1978, over 40% of all first marriages in the U.S. and 54% of all second marriages were ending in divorce. And the rates continue to climb. As a result, studies show, the number of single-parent families in the U.S. has increased 71% in the last 30 years.

A major factor underlying these statistics is the spread of a selfist "me first" attitude on the part of husbands and wives. It is also demonstrated in the attitudes of parents towards children. Children are increasingly perceived as undesirable nuisances, obstacles to the couple's freedom. Evidence of this can be seen in the Supreme Court's 1973 ruling on abortion, and the consequent explosion of abortion statistics in recent years.

The overwhelming evidence of the impact of the gospel of selfism on family life in our society is not to be seen merely in charts, graphs, and impersonal statistics. It can be found all around us, fashionably displayed in the lives of many people we know. Take, for instance, a young university professor I met a short while ago. It was a balmy summer evening, and we were chatting on the front porch of his house, while his two very active and fun-loving boys frolicked together in the front yard. The subject of our beliefs came up, and as he did not profess to be a Christian, I asked him to explain his philosophy of life. "It's really pretty simple," he said. "I live for myself." He hooked his thumb toward his sons, who were wrestling and laughing in the grass. "You know, I love my kids. They're really a lot of fun. But I'll tell you straight out, if it ever comes to an issue of them or me . . . " He paused and poked his chest decisively with his thumb. "It's gonna be me." I was appalled, but not surprised. He was only asserting more boldly a set of values held by many others who would be ashamed to admit them so blatantly.

A friend of mine told me of another instance of such attitudes he encountered recently. He and his wife were speaking together in a small café, and in the booth behind them, two young women began carrying on an animated discussion. It was loud enough that my friend could not help overhearing parts of the conversation. "I'm still undecided about whether Joe and I should have children. I mean, on the one hand, I think I'd find it very enjoyable and satisfying. On the other hand, it seems so restrictive. I think I might feel stifled in my growth as a person to be so tied down to someone else. I guess I'm not sure if I'd feel fulfilled by having children. And if it's not fulfilling—man, I'd really be stuck."

My friend, who has some children of his own, and knows very well what it means to be a parent, shook his head and said to himself, "Lady, if all you'd be in it for is personal fulfillment, please do yourself and the world a favor and don't have any children."

The family is not the only place where we see the disturbing inroads of the selfist gospel. To a startling degree, selfism has also corrupted the minds of today's youth. Many of the young, traditionally among society's most high-minded, sacrificial, and idealistic individuals, are today almost totally absorbed in themselves, their own pleasure, and their future.

Lansing Lamont, a former *Time* bureau chief, comments on the plunge into self-concern taken by university students in *Campus Shock*, an eye-opening report on the sad state of affairs on the most prestigious university campuses of the 1970s.

> They fought each other—sometimes physically—not only for grades, jobs and coveted graduate school positions, but for financial aid, choice housing, even the books on reserve in the overused libraries. "You understand that everybody is your enemy," wrote a young Harvard M.B.A., "and you learn to fear and hate people, to live in crowded isolation."

Selfism Versus Servanthood: God's Great Reversal

To summarize, when examined against the Christian standard of the two greatest commandments, the gospel of selfism utterly fails the test. It comes as no surprise, then, that it does no better with Jesus' teaching on servanthood. Once again, it squares off against the basics of the Christian gospel. And wherever the spirit of the gospel of selfism prevails, the words of Jesus seem patently absurd, childishly naive, and very hard to take. "Humble yourself like a child." "Become like a slave." "Wash one another's feet." Jesus does not speak about being "self-actualized" or "fulfilled" in this life. In fact, quite the opposite. He earnestly insists, "If any man would come after me, let him deny himself and take up his cross daily and follow me. For whoever would save his life will lose it; and whoever loses his life for my sake, he will save it" (Lk 9:23-24).

When Jesus says, "deny yourself," he isn't merely speaking of some simple practices of "self-denial." Rather, "to deny" is a term that describes a relationship with someone. It means "to renounce a claim upon." Jesus demands that any who would be his disciples must renounce their own claims upon their lives. "Stop acting like your life is yours, to do with as you please or as you find fulfilling. If you will follow me, your life is no longer yours, but mine."

Often, Jesus' words seem hard to fathom and difficult to apply. At first hearing, worldly wisdom carries a ring of truth. It is certainly fair to say that in our world the philosophy of the survival of the fittest, and even of "doing unto others before they can do unto us," seems to make good sense. Many of these attitudes and approaches to life have long characterized the human population (ever since the Fall!). We can hardly expect much better from our own society.

But we can and should expect something quite different from God's people. Though here, sadly, we are often disappointed. Many Christians today have written off Jesus' "hard-to-handle" words and have swallowed the contemporary gospel of selfism. Sometimes they propagate selfist doctrines as enthusiastically and vigorously as any of the secular advocates. They seem oblivious to the fact that the gospel of selfism fundamentally opposes Jesus' own teaching. This development among modern Christians is extremely unfortunate because Jesus' words on the matter are clear, forceful, and uncompromising.

Remember Jesus' words, "He who exalts himself shall be humbled." Here is a clear, stern warning for all Christians. God does not want his people to put themselves, their interests, or their personal fulfillment first. He is not pleased that large numbers of his flock follow the seductive voice of another master. Jesus tells us plainly that those who put themselves first will be cut down to size. Then he goes on: "He who humbles himself will be exalted." God himself will honor and exalt those who put their trust in him when in a lowly position as well as those who purposely take on an attitude and a posture of lowliness in obedience to his instructions. This paradoxical pattern has always characterized God's way of working with his people. As Paul puts it: "God chose what is foolish in the world to shame the wise, God chose what is weak in the world to shame the strong, God chose what is low and despised in the world, even things that are not, to bring to nothing things that are, so that no human being might boast in the presence of God" (1 Cor 1:27-29).

This was God's way with Abraham, the simple and obedient man whose faith found favor in God's sight. As he humbled himself in obedience before God, God exalted him to wealth and prosperity, and to everlasting greatness as the "father of many nations."

The humble trust of the righteous in their God was a vital lesson taught to the Israelites as they became a nation. God humbled the proud and haughty Egyptian oppressors by his own power, and lifted up the children of Israel to a unique status among all the nations on earth: to be a royal priesthood, God's own people.

Again and again, God dealt with his people in this way, and taught them this lesson through the prophets (see Is 29:19-20) and other writings of the Old Testament. The psalms take up this theme and repeat it often.

> You save the humble but bring low those whose eyes are haughty (Ps 18:27).

> Love the Lord, all you his saints! The Lord preserves the faithful, but abundantly requites him who acts haughtily (Ps 31:23).

> For though the Lord is high, he regards the lowly; but the haughty he knows from afar.
> (Ps 138:6).

The New Testament continues the message of this "great reversal" even more strongly than in the Old Testament. At the revelation of God's plan of salvation, Mary proclaims in the Magnificat:

He has scattered the proud in the imagination of their hearts, he has put down the mighty from their thrones, and exalted those of low degree; he has filled the hungry with good things, and the rich he has sent empty away (Lk 1:51-53).

In the coming of Jesus, God has once again turned the tables, bringing down the stiff-necked and proud and exalting those who humbly trust in him. The New Testament teaches that Christians should model themselves after Jesus, who humbled himself as a slave and was exalted by his Father (Phil 2:5-11). "Humble yourselves before the Lord and he will exalt you" (Jas 4:10). "Humble yourselves therefore under the mighty hand of God, that in due time he may exalt you" (1 Pt 5:6).

The Beatitudes

This lesson is stated most clearly and powerfully by Jesus himself in the Sermon on the Mount, particularly in the Beatitudes. The Beatitudes are Jesus' first words in the Sermon on the Mount. Although spoken in the presence of the crowd, they are intended by Jesus as instruction for his disciples. Each Beatitude begins with "Blessed are . . ." (or to put it another way, "How truly fortunate are . . ."). Then it goes on to describe a certain spiritual condition that the disciples should have and the results that will flow from that condition. There are eight main Beatitudes (the ninth is an elaboration of the eighth). The first four have a certain relationship to one another, and to the second four. A good look at the first and third Beatitudes will reveal how God's "great reversal" appears at the center of Jesus' teaching.

The first four Beatitudes address the disciples' relationship with God. Each of them describes an attitude or a posture before God that involves voluntary personal deprivation, expressing love for God and trust in him. The first Beatitude says, "Blessed [or "How fortunate"] are the poor in spirit, for theirs is the kingdom of heaven." Jesus is not speaking primarily of those without material wealth, for many who are materially poor are far from being "fortunate." He is speaking rather of his disciples, who do not rely simply upon themselves for what they need. They are to live in a state of trust and reliance upon God, looking to him to provide for them. As they do so, they will receive everything they need—the fullness of his kingdom. His teaching echoes a theme often found in the psalms, where the righteous who trust in the Lord are referred to as the "poor." The spiritual condition that Jesus calls for in his disciples is one of deep and abiding faith in God. It is a condition that causes one to rely on God's grace. Such trust should not be confused with irresponsibility or passivity.

The third Beatitude is closely related to the first. "Blessed are the meek, for they shall inherit the earth." Jesus' words state succinctly the same lesson he is to give his disciples on the road to Jerusalem. "How fortunate," says Jesus, "are those who take on an attitude of lowliness, the posture of a servant, for they will receive from God their promised inheritance." Here again, Jesus is teaching directly from the Psalms. In this case, he quotes Psalm 37:11. "But the meek shall possess the land, and delight themselves in abundant prosperity."

Psalm 37 is the prayer of the righteous who are not themselves in a position to overcome the power of the wicked, but who trust in God to provide for them and to deal with their enemies. Its message is expressed well in verses 3-6:

> Trust in the Lord, and do good;
>> so you will dwell in the land, and enjoy
>> security.
> Take delight in the Lord,
>> and he will give you the desires of your
>> heart.
> Commit your way to the Lord;
>> trust in him, and he will act.
> He will bring forth your vindication as the
> light,
>> and your right as the noonday.

The spirit of the first and the third Beatitudes is very similar. In the first, Jesus exhorts his disciples not to depend upon their own resources alone, but to look to God to provide for them. In the third, the issue is one of power and position. The dis-

grasping = power + position

ciples are not to grasp for these things, but are to depend upon God for their power. Jesus assures them that as they put their faith in God and rely upon his grace, they will be fully provided for. Theirs will be the kingdom of heaven; to them will be given the promised inheritance for which they long. Their posture of lowliness and humility before God in reliance upon him opens the way for a special relationship with him, in which God himself can be their all.

Jesus has given his disciples an ideal that was beyond their imagination and understanding. To fallen human nature, especially within the context of the gospel of selfism, this ideal sounds naive and absurd—both impossible and undesirable. But as Paul says (in a different context), "O the depth of the riches and wisdom and knowledge of God! How unsearchable are his judgments and how inscrutable his ways!" (Rm 11:33). The "great reversal" is an inscrutable piece of divine wisdom, which the worldly mind can neither comprehend nor accept; yet blessed are those who understand its message, believe it—and obey.

"If you trust in the Lord and do good,
He'll be right by your side;
If you trust in the Lord and do good,
You'll never have any reason to hide;
You can hold your head up high
and live like a child of the King,
If you trust in the Lord and do good, and do good,
He'll be your everything."

SEVEN

Christian Meekness and Zeal in the Modern World

As we grow in understanding the teaching of scripture on meekness and zeal, we must also try to relate that teaching to the world in which we live. How should this biblical teaching affect our daily behavior? The church's answer is simple and clear: Scripture is the revelation of God. As such, it is the standard by which we must evaluate what is right and wrong, true and false, in the world around us. At times it can be difficult to know how to apply scriptural teaching in today's world. But it is possible, and once we know how to, anything that contradicts or conflicts with scripture's instructions must be judged accordingly, and either rejected or altered in conformity to God's revelation.

How do the meekness and zeal of Christ compare with the prevailing patterns of behavior in our society? In this chapter, we will consider three common ways that people tend to behave, and compare them with the scriptural virtues of meekness and zeal. This will help us to evaluate contemporary patterns in the light of Christian revelation.

The Case of the Inhibited Social Responder

Many people in our society are afflicted with inhibitions about relating to others. These inhibitions can arise from a range of sources, such as shyness, timidity, insecurity, fear, or guilt. They can be expressed differently in different people. Even so, some general observations can be made about the results of such inhibited behavior. Inhibition results in a failure to express oneself effectively to others. This failure can occur both in terms of positive expressions—love, warmth, affection, approval, praise, appreciation, respect—and negative expressions—disagreement, disapproval, anger. It can lead to a pattern of passivity or to an inability to communicate to others what is happening with us.

Unfortunately, inhibited behavior sometimes masquerades as Christian meekness, although it is actually far different from it. This false equation can mislead us into thinking that something which is actually a problem is a virtue. That mistake can prevent us from taking any corrective action. What are some of the symptoms of this inhibited behavior pattern?

A frequent one is the inability to say no when we think we should. A young woman can't say no to the sexual demands of her boyfriend. A mother can't say no to the constant pestering of her children. A businessman can't deny money to an irresponsible friend who is asking for another loan. An overweight man who is trying to cut down can't refuse the "thirds" with which his persistent hostess plies him. Many people fail to give the no that is called for because they fear rejection or because they are manipulated by others to feel guilty or ashamed or because they give in to the constant pressure exerted on them by others.

Another symptom of inhibited behavior is the inability to disagree with others when the situation calls for it. A crusty manager gives directions based on faulty information, but no one has the courage to speak out about it. A professor distorts and ridicules Christianity in his classroom, but no one can summon the nerve to dispute his statements. At times, this failure can have disastrous consequences. A diabolical megalomaniac seized the reins of power in Germany in the 1930s, dragging his country and the rest of the world into the bloodiest war mankind has ever seen. Yet thousands of God-fearing German Christians who opposed Hitler and everything he stood for sat on their hands without opening their mouths, while only a small minority had the courage to speak out against his inhuman atrocities.

Sometimes the freedom to disagree when necessary only involves the ability to speak one's mind. At other times, it can take great courage to speak out and "face the music" for doing so. Such freedom is inherent in the character of Jesus. The failure to speak out does not represent true Christian meekness.

A third symptom of inhibited behavior is the tendency to repress anger instead of expressing it appropriately. A secretary's boss chews her out for an error she did not commit. She remains silent, despite the anger welling up within her, and is in a state of turmoil for the rest of the afternoon. She complains to a friend in the next office, but does nothing about setting the matter straight with her boss. A student waits with mounting irritation for his lab partner, who finally shows up forty-five minutes late with a lame excuse. Rather than discussing the matter straightforwardly, the irritated student gives his partner an icy reception, remaining cool and aloof throughout the experiment. Lacking the freedom to express our anger in a proper and healthy way is not a Christian virtue. Generally the anger will still come out, as in the above examples, but will be expressed less constructively. Unhealthy repression is not a characteristic of Christian meekness.

One further symptom of inhibited behavior worth mentioning here is the failure to give firm direction and make it stick when we are responsible for something. A young teacher calls for quiet from her unruly seventh-grade class. Her students have learned, however, that nothing will back up her words. She never follows through on her threats. As a result, chaos reigns in the classroom. After careful consideration a father announces to his children that he does not want them to watch television on school nights. He is met with a chorus of protests, and after a brief skirmish, he backs down and lets them do what they want. A governor makes a decision about an issue, then changes his mind, changes it again, and then a third time as different interest groups pressure him about his position. Christian meekness does not condone rigidity or harshness in authority, but it does require firmness and a capacity to insist on what is right. Always giving in to others when we are in authority is not a sign of meekness.

Many other symptoms could be described, but these four are enough to make the point. There is a world of difference between inhibited social behavior and Christian meekness. Meekness is not passive, nor is it inhibited. It arises from strength, not from weakness, and it is based on a servant-like response to the situation at hand. The meekness of Jesus left him free to say no, to disagree strenuously, to show his anger, and to take a firm stand when the occasion warranted it.

The Case of the Overly Aggressive Responder

Others in our society have exhibited a very different behavioral pattern. Some have fully adopted what might be called a "jungle mentality." It runs like this: "It's a jungle out there, and the ground rules are 'the survival of the fittest' and 'nice guys finish last.'" Many people have learned how to get what they want by the aggressive use of force—whether the force of personality, of strongly stated opinion, of emotional manipulation, of pressure tactics, or of physical coercion.

While it has always been true that some members of any population or culture will be extremely aggressive and domineering, it has become a consciously chosen style in our Western society, adopted by many who want to get their own way at others' expense. In many cases, this behavior was first learned from movements where it was developed as a political style—especially movements that came out of the "New Left" (often inspired in their analyses and tactics by Marxist methods): student activism, black power, women's liberation, gay liberation. Methods that employ aggressive confrontation strongly expressed opinion and emotion, intimidation, and pressure tactics, originally developed in political settings, have become personal tools for individuals who see personal relationships primarily in terms of what they can gain from them. Whatever one may think of their validity as political tactics, these methods have no place in a Christian approach to personal relationships. The success of these domineering individuals is compounded by the problem of the "inhibited social responders," who do not cope effectively with this sort of overbearing, manipulative behavior, and who therefore are easy marks to be taken advantage of.

An aggressive, often domineering behavior that aims at benefitting oneself at the expense of others bears practically no resemblance to Christian zeal, except on the most superficial levels. By nature, they are entirely different species, springing from different sources, employed for different purposes, expressed in different ways, and resulting in very different effects on other people.

Assertiveness Training

The behavior patterns of the "inhibited social responders" and the "overly aggressive responders" are not only unacceptable from the viewpoint of Christian meekness and zeal, but inadequate as healthy human behavior patterns. In recognition of the problems inherent in these two patterns, a movement of thought has emerged in the field of psychology which has been widely popularized over the last decade. It is commonly called "Assertiveness Training," although it has also been called "assertive therapy," "personal effectiveness training," and "social skills training." It aims to help people cope effectively with the problems and pressures of relating to others in today's increasingly complex society. In its most useful forms, it attempts to offer a third alternative, a middle way between inhibited responders and overly aggressive responders.

Assertiveness training techniques are generally offered from an entirely secular position. They offer a fair dose of worldly wise advice, some of which can be very profitably employed by Christians. The fact that it has value if properly used makes it all the more important to subject the whole assertiveness-training approach to the scrutiny of the Christian mind—examining its values, presuppositions, and advice in the light of Christian truth.

It's important to note that wide diversity exists within assertiveness training. Some of its popularizers are balanced and prudent and show a high degree of concern for ethical behavior and for safeguarding the rights of others. On the other hand, some writers demonstrate very little ethical concern, offering techniques for intimidating and manipulating others. This latter category, far from providing any real solution to the inadequacies of the first two behavior types, actually contributes to the problem.

In this analysis, we will examine the strengths and weaknesses of assertiveness training from the Christian perspective by using one of the most balanced and respected popular books in the field: *Your Perfect Right*, by Robert Alberti and Michael Emmons. Then we will refer to other, less ethically-attuned approaches.

Alberti and Emmons distinguish their ideal of "assertive" behavior from behavior which is "non-assertive" (what we call "inhibited") and from that which is "aggressive" (what we termed "overly aggressive"). According to their definition, "assertive" behavior is "behavior which enables a person to act in his or her own best interests, to stand up for herself or himself without undue anxiety, to express honest feelings comfortably, or to exercise personal rights without denying the rights of others."[8] We can already see from the preliminary definition that the framework of assertiveness training is a secular one—a primary concern for one's own best interests and one's personal rights.

Besides definitions, the authors offer numerous examples of the three types of behavior, which are very useful in fleshing out their concept of assertiveness. In this example, (a) is "non-assertive",

(b) is "aggressive", and (c) is the proper "assertive" response.

"One of your subordinates has been coming in late consistently for the last three or four days.

Alternative responses:

(a) You grumble to yourself or to others about the situation, but say nothing to the person, hoping he will start coming in early.

(b) You tell the worker off, indicating that he has no right to take advantage of you and that he had better get to work on time or else you will see that he is fired.

(c) Approaching the worker, you point out that you have observed him coming in late recently and wonder if there is an explanation. If he does not have a legitimate excuse, you say firmly that he should start coming to work on time. If the excuse seems legitimate you still say that he should have come to you and explained the situation rather than saying nothing at all, leaving you "up in the air."[9]

The Strengths of Assertiveness Training

One of assertiveness training's main strengths is that it puts a finger on bona fide behavioral problems and offers useful insight into those problems. Many people today are afflicted with inhibited, non-assertive behavior, which makes them unnecessarily subject to people and circumstances around them. Many others exhibit overly aggressive behavior that makes them hard to live with.

Furthermore, at least in its better forms, assertiveness training not only recognizes the problems, it offers practical advice that often squares with Christian behavior patterns. First, it advocates dealing with conflict in controlled strength—not in weakness nor in an uncontrolled manner. The motivation given (standing up for one's own rights) is far different than that of Christian meekness (being God's servant), but the recommended behavior pattern is actually quite similar.

Second, it recognizes that not all anger is wrong, and that anger can and should be expressed in a healthy and constructive way. This notion is reflected in the New Testament, where Paul instructs the Ephesians, "Be angry but do not sin. Do not let the sun go down on your anger" (Eph 4:26).

Third, it recognizes the need for a healthy expression of love, praise, and encouragement in personal relationships.

Fourth, it highlights the importance of straightforwardness in communication, rather than indirectness and inexpressiveness. Being free to say what should be said, directly and honestly, is a Christian virtue *as long as it serves the situation to do so*. Of course, assertiveness training does not tend to be very attuned to this vital qualification.

Despite the very different presuppositions and motivations offered, assertiveness training's specific suggestions, at least in the form given by

Alberti and Emmons, can be quite useful to the discerning Christian.

The Weaknesses of Assertiveness Training

It is precisely in the presuppositions that undergird assertiveness training that its weaknesses and problems for a Christian come into focus. We will mention a few of its major flaws.

First, like much of psychology, assertiveness training is very "selfist" in focus. It therefore fails dismally on the test of the two greatest commandments, completely missing the love of God and distorting the love of neighbor. It also manifests many of the other problems characteristic of the "selfist" mentality.

Second, its values are a far cry from God's standards for righteousness. In fact, most advocates of assertiveness training believe that values are entirely relative, a matter of one's own choice (as long as no one gets hurt, many will add).

Third, assertiveness training operates on a very different notion of equality than does the New Testament. Its modern "equal means identical" approach ends up leveling important social roles based on age, sex, and position, which are an integral part of New Testament instruction on personal relationships. The loss of these could ultimately be a source of grave disorder in the family, between husbands and wives, parents and children.

This description is of assertiveness training at its

best. However, it does get worse. If Alberti and Emmons display moral relativism, Manuel Smith's *When I Say No, I Feel Guilty* advocates a complete moral vacuum. Smith offers a "bill of assertive rights," the first of which makes his overall position quite clear. He says, "Let's examine, first, our prime assertive right . . . from which all the other assertive rights are derived: *our right to be the ultimate judge of all we are and all we do*."[10] Smith draws out the implications of this "right" a bit further on: "*Shoulds*, as a rule of thumb, can be categorized as manipulative structure used to get you to do what someone else wants or arbitrary structure you have imposed on yourself to deal with your own insecurity concerning what you "can and cannot" do. . . . Whenever you hear yourself or someone else say "should," extend your antimanipulative antennae up as far as possible and listen carefully. In all likelihood, some message that says, 'You are not your own judge,' will follow."[11]

As the cover proclaims, Smith's book is "the bestseller with revolutionary techniques for getting your own way." Needless to say, Smith's more blatantly amoral and fiercely selfist approach to assertiveness training makes his book of less value for Christian adaptation than that of Alberti and Emmons.

At its best, assertiveness training is a mixed bag, from which a thoughtful Christian must pick and choose carefully. At its worst, it should be avoided entirely. In general, while some of the assertive skills, techniques, and practices can be of value if properly adapted, much of the overarching framework of values and view of life is very foreign and contrary to a Christian perspective and must be rejected. If done wisely, a Christian can extract what is good from it in order to strongly (and assertively) love God and neighbor, take on the mind of a servant, and live righteously according to God's commandments.

EIGHT

Putting It All Together

As we have studied the nature of Christian meekness and zeal, comparing them with today's dominant secular ideals and behavior patterns, a consistent assumption has been that these apparently contradictory Christian virtues are actually like two sides of the same coin. Responding in both of these ways at different times need not be an exercise in schizophrenia. What is more, we have held that these two traits not only can go together—they *must* go together if a Christian is truly to become like the Lord. In this last chapter, we will consider how a Christian can combine meekness and zeal in order to more closely resemble the character of Christ.

For the total picture to be right, it can often be necessary for two seemingly contradictory elements of behavior to exist side by side. The "contradiction" may only be apparent, deriving from a misunderstanding of one or both of the elements involved. I learned this important lesson during my boyhood.

I had the great fortune to be born to wise Christian parents who clearly understood a principle that many modern parents have utterly lost: that to

love one's child and to discipline that child are not
contradictory practices, but are two sides of the
same coin. It was not a lesson I learned in the
abstract, but through years of experience. You
might even say that I learned it in the "school of
hard knocks," because it took more than a few
hard knocks from my parents to drill that lesson
home. My parents gave us a great deal of love and
affection, making sure that we had all we needed
and more, praising and encouraging us when we
did well. But while that love and affection characterized my relationship with them, I learned that I
could expect a sharp scolding or a resounding
whack for transgressing their rules and directions.
Even so, the punishment was administered fairly,
often with an explanation and assurance of love.
As a result, it alway has made sense to me that
love and discipline, which many people today
think of as opposites, go hand in hand.

I learned the same lesson from the other end of
the relationship as a somewhat older boy. As I
reached the end of grade school, one of my greatest desires came true—our family finally got a dog.
I was ecstatic. As the oldest boy in our family,
much of the responsibility for training and caring
for that puppy fell to me. As we began to house-
train her, my father taught me the importance of
disciplining her if she were to learn. As much as I
loved that little dog, I needed to have the internal
freedom to be angry when she did something
wrong (even if sometimes I had to hide a smile at
her antics), and to administer yesterday's sports
page to her hindquarters with appropriate gusto

when she deserved it. It was very educational, for both of us. I learned what it means to put love and discipline together, indeed how they function naturally side by side.

The same relationship exists between meekness and zeal. If we don't appreciate the connection, we can end up trying our utmost to be meek, humble, and kind, but in doing so, toss out the important counterbalancing virtue of aggressive zeal. This mistake can make us "nice," "gentle" people who lead a version of Christian life that is softer and weaker than it should be. As a result, we could find ourselves being "meek" and "gentle" when the appropriate godly response is to be aggressively zealous. A careful look at the life of Jesus makes it clear that he wasn't just a friendly, harmless, "nice guy." There were certain occasions on which he was anything but nice (Lk 11, Mt 23). Of course the opposite error is also a danger—throwing out meekness in favor of constant zeal, and finding ourselves incapable of the courtesy, forbearance, and humility of Christ when it is called for. We should seek the development of our natural and spiritual instincts in such a way that we learn to respond to each circumstance according to the nature of God within us—being meek when meekness is proper and zealous when zeal is the appropriate response.

A Useful Distinction

An important distinction can help us to uncover a principle governing the interaction of meekness and zeal: the difference between a *commandment* and a *character trait*. A commandment of God is absolute. It does not vary from one situation to the next. For instance, the commandment "Thou shalt not commit adultery" is not subject to changes of time, place, or culture. There is no proviso that adds "unless between two consenting adults," or "unless your spouse has agreed to an 'open marriage,'" or "unless you sincerely love each other." The commandment is simple, clear, and final; it does not change with changing circumstances.

A character trait, on the other hand, will be expressed differently in different circumstances. Meekness and zeal are two of the many elements of the nature of God, and therefore of God's children. Christians are not always to be gentle and forbearing, nor are they always to act out of aggressive zeal. As does God himself, we will vary our responses as the conditions require.

In his first letter to the Corinthians, Paul gives us an excellent example of manifesting different character traits according to the circumstances. After admonishing the Corinthians for their boasting, he issues a warning:

Some are arrogant, as though I were not coming to you. But I will come to you soon, if the Lord wills, and I will find out not the talk of these arrogant people but their power. For the kingdom of God does not consist in talk but in power. What do you wish? Shall I come to you with a rod, or with love in a spirit of gentleness? [literally, "meekness"] (1 Cor 4:18-21).

"In other words," Paul says, "you have a choice about how I will come to you. My preference is to come in a spirit of meekness and love, but if your behavior requires it, you will instead see my aggressive zeal. I will respond as the situation demands." This seems to be a message that is slow to penetrate the Corinthians' minds, because Paul has to protest his readiness to come with anger and zeal in his second letter as well.

I, Paul, myself entreat you, by the meekness and gentleness of Christ—I who am humble when face to face with you, but bold to you when I am away!—I beg of you that when I am present I may not have to show boldness with such confidence as I count on showing against some who suspect us of acting in a worldly fashion. For though we live in the world we are not carrying on a worldly war, for the weapons of our warfare are not worldly but have divine power to destroy strongholds. We destroy arguments and every proud obstacle to the knowledge of God, and take every thought captive to obey Christ, being ready to punish every disobedience, when your obedience is complete (2 Cor 10:1-6).

When to Do What?

If then, following the example of Paul, our response in manifesting different traits of Christian character varies with the circumstances, what guiding principle do we use? Here it would help to recall the broader context of our discussion of meekness and zeal throughout this book. Both of these qualities have been seen to point beyond themselves to an even broader and more fundamental quality: Christian servanthood. We have noted that meekness epitomizes this servant-like aspect of Christ's own character, but that Christ-like servanthood cannot be fully understood apart from the counterbalancing quality of zeal. Grasping this broader context of Christian servanthood can provide us with an important guiding principle: *Our Christian response to the different circumstances which confront us should not be formed by our emotional reactions or by our preferences, but by what will best serve the Lord and the people around us.* Exercising true meekness and zeal, then, requires us to have the freedom from ourselves and our own immediate reactions to respond to our circumstances in whatever way is best: freedom to obey and be gentle in one situation, and freedom from fear and self-concern in order to be properly aggressive and zealous in another.

Once we are clear about this fundamental principle, it is primarily a matter of applying God's wisdom and teaching to determine what is right and what will best serve the situation at hand. This task is easier said than done. In fact, it is often quite difficult. Various sticky issues can present themselves to us as we attempt to understand and apply God's wisdom. It would require a far longer book, one that was broader in scope, to tackle all the questions and issues involved, and we must content ourselves here with a few general principles that can help point the way.

1. In those matters in which *our* claims, rights, preferences, and ways of doing things are at stake, we should act meekly. That is, we should be courteous, gentle, forbearing, and ready to accomodate the wishes of others rather than to insist on our own. This principle seems to be the point of Jesus' challenging command in the Sermon on the Mount:

> You have heard that it was said, "An eye for an eye and a tooth for a tooth." But I say to you, Do not resist one who is evil. But if any one stikes you on the right cheek, turn to him the other also; and if any one would sue you and take your coat, let him have your cloak as well; and if any one forces you to go one mile, go with him two miles (Mt 5:38-41).

Here Jesus describes three occasions for showing meekness in response to personal offenses. First, striking someone on the right cheek with the back of the right hand was considered a very serious form of insult. By instructing his disciples to turn the other cheek, Jesus is not saying, "Let people beat you up," but, "Do not retaliate when you are personally insulted, but bear it in meekness." He then goes on to mention two other occasions: when our possessions are taken from us and when our time and energy are demanded.

Again his direction is to forbear and to avoid retaliation. It would be possible to interpret and apply Jesus' words in a way that leads to the timidity, weakness, and passivity of Marvin Milksop, but that distorts his intentions. Jesus is not teaching Christians to be naive or to lie down and let others walk on them or to passively allow others to take advantage of them. Nor do his words necessarily eliminate all forms of self-defense and protection of property and reputation. Nor does he command us to completely ignore or deny our own preferences and claims. Yet he certainly points out that our behavior ought to be characterized by meekness when it comes to our claims, rights, and preferences—a willingness to lay them down when it will serve him or those around us.

2. On the other hand, when *God's* claims, rights, and preferences are at stake—when it is a matter of standing for what is good, right, true, and just—then a godly boldness, aggressiveness, and zeal should characterize our response. This principle applies to our efforts to evangelize others, defend the helpless, and discipline those for whom the Lord has given us responsibility (eg., our children). Of course, godly zeal is not free license for boldness and aggression. Our zeal is to be tempered by meekness; it is expressed without malice, hatred, revenge, or quarreling (see 2 Tm 2:23-26).

A young Christian friend of mine is a good example of this kind of godly zeal. He was sitting with some friends of his one evening, and one of them began to mock the Bible and certain basic Christian truths. My friend didn't simply sit there passively, nor did he join in the laughter of the group. He didn't haul off and belt the guy in the mouth, or begin mocking him or calling him names, either. He simply let some righteous anger show as he pointed to the offender and said, "That's not funny, Joe. I don't want to hear that kind of thing any more." The others respected him enough to stop their mocking. And their respect for him grew because of his stand.

as a c.o.!

3. When we have been entrusted with authority and leadership, greater firmness and zeal may be called for than in situations in which we do not exercise authority. For example, as parents, our relationship with our own children will have a stronger proportion of determined, aggressive zeal in it (a zeal for their proper training and for their righteous behavior) than would our relationships with other kids in the neighborhood. We could state this principle even more broadly: even when it is not a matter of exercising a clear leadership role we should be zealous in carrying out any responsibility we have before God. This principle holds true whether we speak of parents with responsibilities for their families and jobs, or students with school responsibilities, or Christian leaders who are responsible for the direction of their groups. Wherever God places us, whatever he has us doing at any particular time, we should be zealous to see that our responsibilities are faithfully fulfilled. Surely this is the mark of a good and faithful servant.

When it comes to being meek or zealous, we should do whatever will best serve those around us to move them toward the Lord and closer to the truth. One common occasion that calls for deciding on whether to be meek or zealous occurs in evangelism. Sometimes a strong and bold explanation of the gospel will be most effective. However, at other times, coming on strong can have a negative effect, making a person more hostile and less open to Christianity. Instead, a more patient, gentle, and persevering approach to the same person may be what helps them advance toward the truth.

Learning to be both meek and zealous, then, does not require that we develop a split personality. It does not mean being timid, mild-mannered Clark Kent at one moment and brave, gallant Superman the next. Rather, it means learning to put two Christian character traits together in a manner that mirrors God's own character—choosing to respond to our every circumstance with the same love, service, and strength that Jesus would in our place.

Conclusion

It's Our Choice

Long ago, perhaps before time ever was, the first sin of the universe was committed by the highest being in all creation. The sinner was Lucifer. The sin was pride. At a certain point, Lucifer rebelled against God and rejected his authority. "No," said he, "I will not serve. I will not obey." Herein lies the sin of pride: not, as many think, in an overly exalted opinion of oneself, but in the refusal to serve. This was the same sin with which Satan would eventually tempt and ensnare our first parents, promising that they, too, could be like God, no longer needing to serve and obey him.

Much later, in the fullness of time, the Son of God himself took flesh and became man. He came in meekness and humility. He came as a servant. "Father, not my will but yours be done." "The son of man came not to be served, but to serve."

When all is said and done, a clear-cut choice lies before us. Meekness and zeal, qualities of being a servant, are fundamental to the character and identity of Jesus. Pride, the refusal to serve, is inherent in the character of Satan. The posture we take toward being a servant and our ability to take on true Christian meekness and zeal will have much to say about who we come to resemble in the final analysis.

The character of Jesus also reveals more fully the character of the Father. He who rules the universe, who commands all power in heaven and on earth, deigns to be meek and humble toward us. While at the proper time his zeal and his wrath can break out in great force, God's primary posture towards us is that of love and service. He has revealed his own meekness most completely in the sending of his only son for our salvation, in the role of a servant, with a servant's character. May we also learn the character of Jesus, the meek and zealous servant of the Lord, that we might become true children of our Father in heaven, bearing the very stamp of his nature.

in response to His standards of truth and righteousness (p. 124, #2)

Notes

1. C. S. Lewis, *Mere Christianity* (New York: Macmillan Co., 1943), p. 174.

2. Ibid., p. 155.

3. For a brief and valuable discussion of this Greek term, two of William Barclay's works are especially recommended: *New Testament Words* (Philadelphia: Westminster Press, 1974), pp. 240-242; *Flesh and Spirit* (Nashville: Abingdon Press, 1962), pp. 111-121.

4. J.B. Phillips, *Your God Is Too Small* (New York: Macmillan Co., 1961), pp. 27-28.

5. Richard Wurmbrand, *Tortured for Christ* (Old Tappan, New Jersey: Spire, Fleming H. Revell Co., 1969), pp. 57-58, 66.

6. Paul Vitz, *Psychology As Religion: The Cult of Self-Worship* (Grand Rapids, Michigan: Wm. B. Eerdmans Publishing Co., 1977), pp. 32-33.

7. Lansing Lamont, *Campus Shock: A First-Hand Report on Student Life at America's Leading Universities* (New York: E.P. Dutton, 1979), p. 3.

8. Robert E. Alberti and Michael L. Emmons, *Your Perfect Right: A Guide to Assertive Behavior*, 3rd ed. rev. (San Luis Obispo, California: Impact Pubs., Inc., 1978), p. 2.

9. Ibid., pp. 113-114.

10. Manuel Smith, *When I Say No, I Feel Guilty* (New York: Dial Press, 1975), p. 28.

11. Ibid., p. 70-71.